GW01606613

True art makes the divine silence in the Soul
break into applause.

Sufi Mystic-Hafiz

FIONA ALMELEH

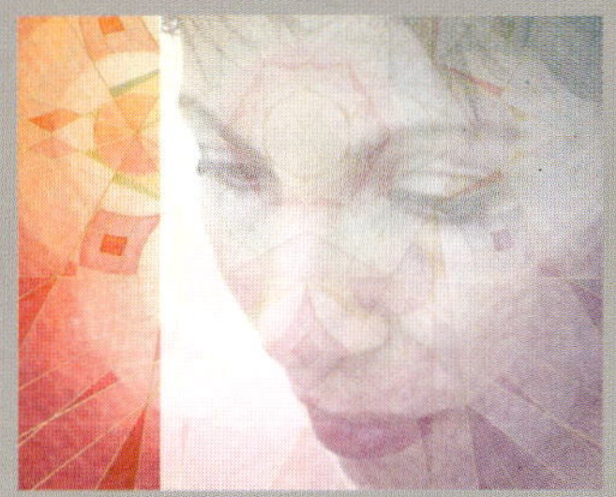

TRUE COLOURS

A creative exploration into the worlds of light and colour

Produced by Fiona Almeleh
E-mail:almeleh@iafrica.com
P.O. Box 31284 Tokai 7966
ISBN 0-620-29907-X

The illustrations in this book are reproductions from the original paintings by Fiona Almeleh

First published 2002

Published and printed in South Africa
by Fiona Almeleh

Cover design and layout by Warren Nelson

Edited by Carol Nelson

THE WORK OF FIONA ALMELEH

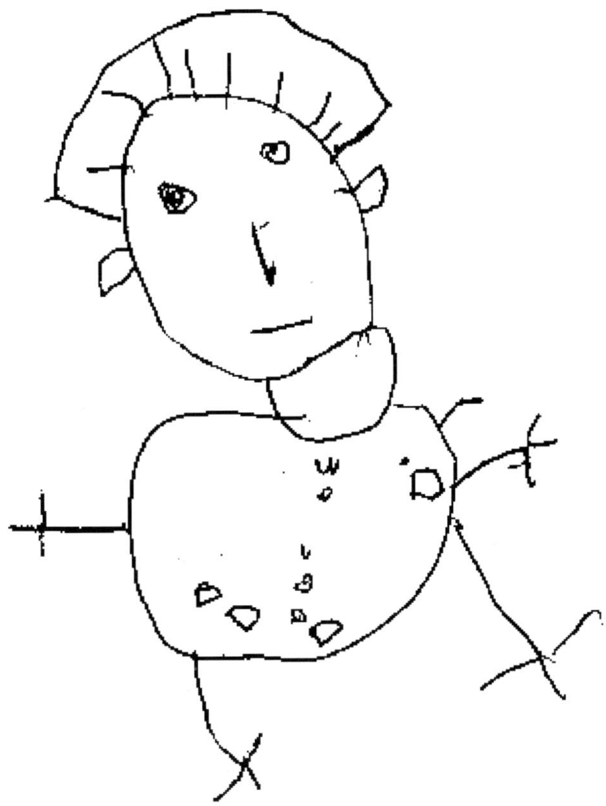

Dedicated to the cherished memory of my sister

Ruth Erna Almeleh

ACKNOWLEDGEMENTS

To my sister Ruthie, without whom I may not have found the courage or the determination to embrace my destiny creatively.

To my beloved parents Judith and Salvo Almeleh, who through their love and support have given me roots that anchor me to the earth and wings to fly to the heavens.

To my children Aaron and Ilana for being my brightest lights and greatest inspiration.

To all those friends, family and the many others who have touched and enriched my life immeasurably.

To all who have so generously given of their time, effort and love in helping me to birth this book.

To Warren, Carol, Simone and Susie

To all beings seen and unseen for their continuing love, support and guidance.

To the Great Spirit.

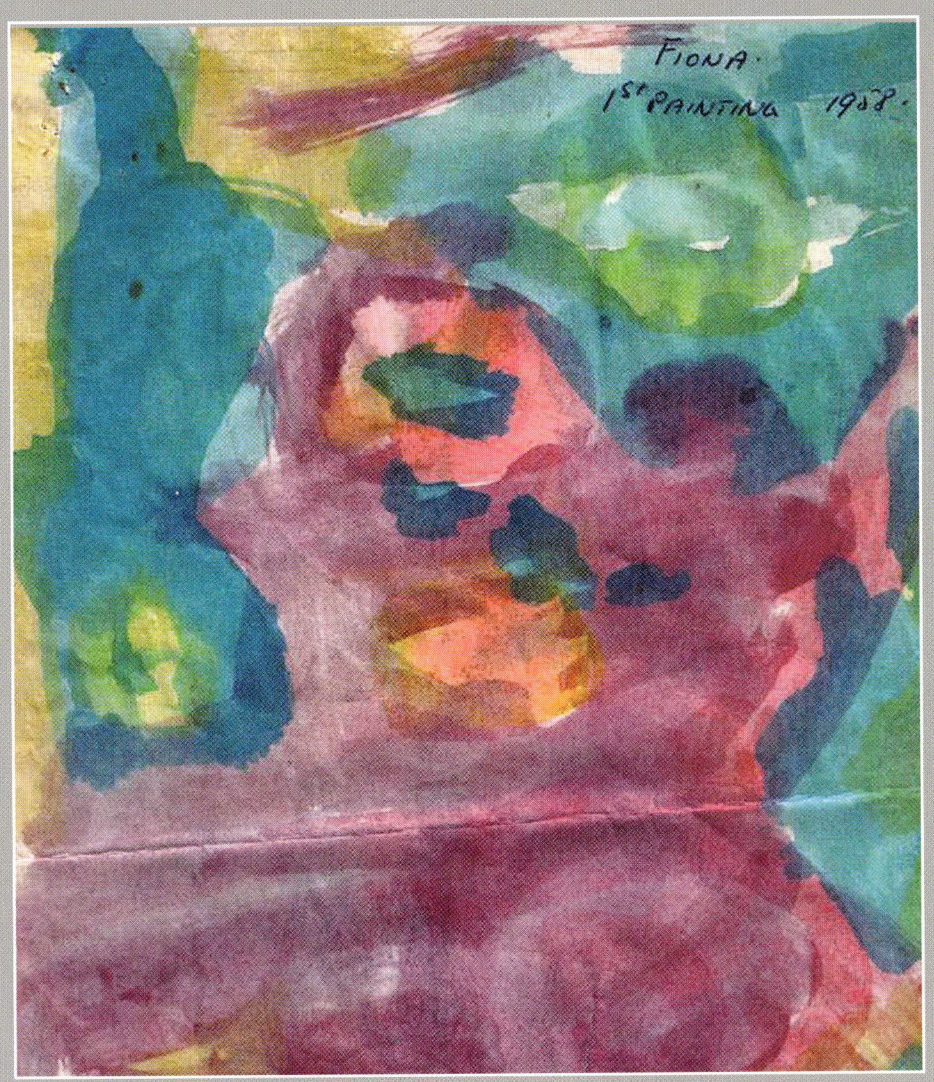
FIONA.
1st PAINTING

FOREWORD

Every now and then I have met a person on my journey through this lifetime who has moved me by the exceptional qualities of spirit that choreograph themselves through their being, qualities such as love, compassion, wise intelligence, inspiration and peace. There is a sense of knowing who they are, where they are going, and that they are at home in themselves. One such person is Fiona Almeleh. She serves others by lifting them to new vision and perception through the light in her eyes and the passion and joy of her being. She is an inspiration, a wise and skilled teacher and an abundantly creative channel for the finest of expression of soul into oil paintings, veil paintings and embroidery sculpture.

As with many creative artists, she has not flinched from exploration into the duality, which is the nature of our experience. She has plummeted the depth of shadow and pain enabling her to take wing into the light of spiritual exploration to translate the subtlest of nuance of meaning and feeling into her image from the world of unconditionally loving spirit. Her creations hold the echo of truth that many strive to make a reality on our planet at this time of evolving consciousness. I refer to the marriage of spirit and matter, bringing light to darkness and density, opening to a reverence and respect for all life forms and recognising the Oneness behind them.

To truly engage with Fiona Almeleh's work is to awaken a distant memory, to surrender to a resonance of soul and spirit, to touch into a deep and rich dance of life where you are transported to a place that reminds you that at some deeper level you are whole, complete, beautiful and powerful. As teacher, she invites you to a deeper exploration of the polarities within you: dark and light, pain and joy, harmony and discord. She beckons you to dance to a more real world where you can discover harmony and balance and where you can become both healed and healer.

Fiona is able to fly as a consummate artist because she has a solid foundation of technical proficiency and has applied her craft diligently and with discipline. It seems this remarkable well-honed skill is the platform from which she is able to let go of an analytical, exterior approach so that the holistic, wise intelligence of the intuition can come through. The power of the visual message is evidence of a spirit of wholeness and sanctity permeating her creations.

Go joyously through these pages. They are the fruit of a great and sensitive talent. Enrich yourself by doing some of the meditations and extend yourself by having fun with the exercises, above all allow your spirit to be moved. Awaken to the dance of love and light through colour!

Natalia Baker-

Metaphysical Teacher and Inspirational Speaker, Cape Town South Africa

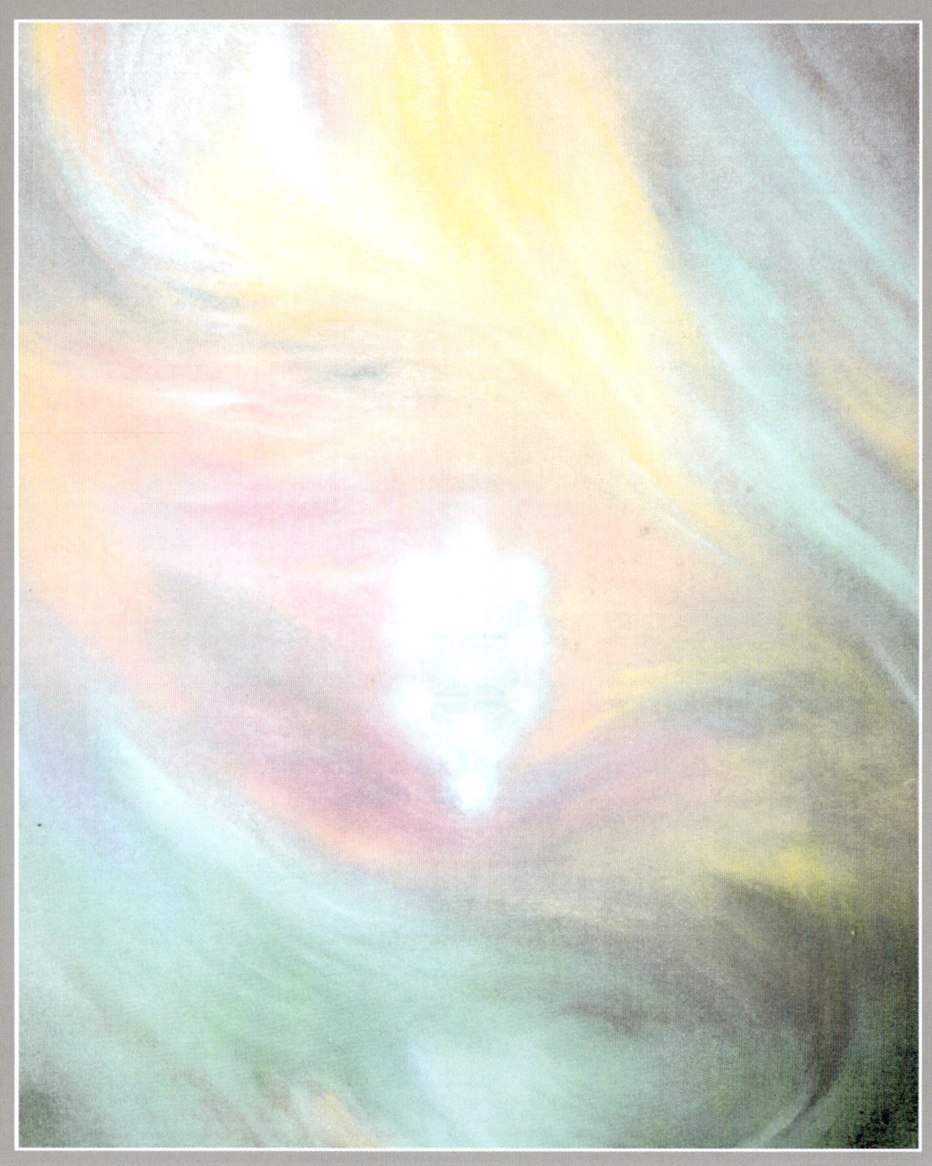

Tree of Life

The symbol of 'Oneness' the 'Tree of Ascension' held in the light of G-ds' love - each step offering us new life, new vision.

CONTENTS

TRUE COLOURS–A creative exploration into the worlds of light and colour

Chances were

A million wings would beat in rhythm
A spirit would rejoice and sing of life's bounty
and we would see the golden thread of connection
appear from the mists of time

We each would become a kaleidoscope of faces
a multitude of expressions and experiences
and we would expand inwardly to embrace limitless realms

Past difficulties would invite new perspectives
G-d would whisper of the greater plan
and joy would dissolve fear and sorrow

The chameleon would inhabit us giving us wider vision
the praying mantis would stand over us as it spoke
the wisdom of our ancestors
and the leopard's glance would melt all resistance
as we surrendered to it's will

Each meeting would call forth our soul's true colours
the distance would become a blessing as it grew us
and the spiritual intimacy would enhance us
We would release the need to understand the unknowable
our separate paths in joining would again reveal great riches
and we would remember to appreciate what we have

This moment - what you believe is true

I know nothing about art, but if I were to sum up my philosophy I would put it thus - when you have regained yourself, all your life becomes the 'artless art' and all your activities must bear the imprint.

Regaining yourself means the merging of a drop in the ocean through the complete annihilation of yourself. Once that happens, you are face to face with the dragon, and You are no more! A bigger power is now seen to wield things and you are just another tool in its hands. The ordinary humdrumness of life is now robed in the extraordinary and phenomenal and life becomes a challenging and wonderful place to live in. Eternity is seen to be in the now and the now is seen to be part of eternity.

Dad

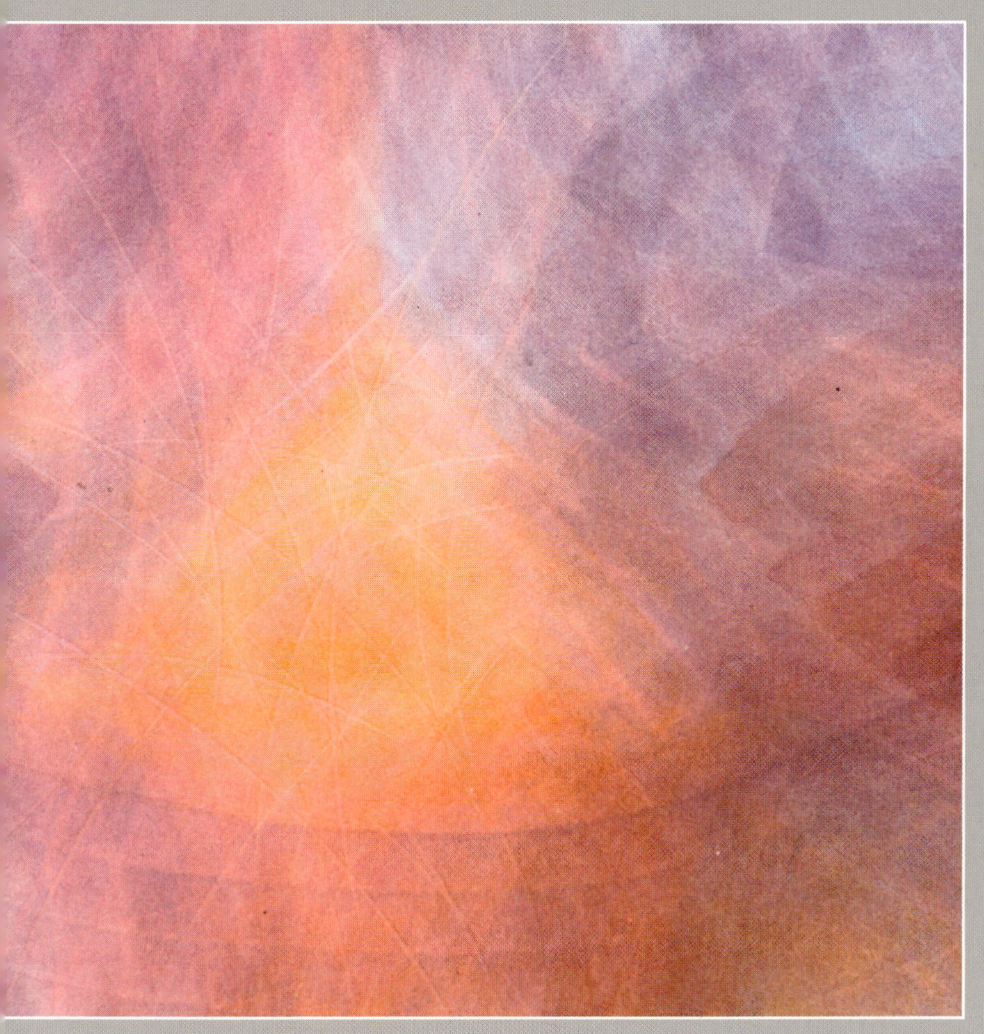

Opening of the Third Eye
The darkness begins to move and clear as we meet truth with open trust and the recognition that we are so much more.

INTRODUCTION

The very nature of love is to entice and beckon us to enter through its sacred gateway into worlds that are filled with wonder and mystery. When we willingly open and surrender to the power of love we see everything as being made of this love and our previously limited perception of the world changes and we have the possibility of becoming all that we can be.

Love is like a magic potion that once drunk leads you into the alchemy of complete transformation.

Rumi

The journey of love has many roads and the one that has called to me the most strongly and persistently has been that of colour and creativity.

Toshumitzu Hasumi in the 'Zen of Japanese Art' describes this process very aptly by saying that,

... it is only when the painter stands brush in hand in front of the canvas before him, does the way to the unique eternal idea open. Creativity through art has a profound operation on the soul.

This is an adventure of both discovering our authenticity and growing to see the world through the eyes of the compassionate observer.

Our first creation is to be ourselves and it is the nature of our creativity to flow freely from our life force. In order to do this requires the spontaneity, imagination and freedom of our inner child. When we open to that which needs expression, we are automatically guided to working intuitively.

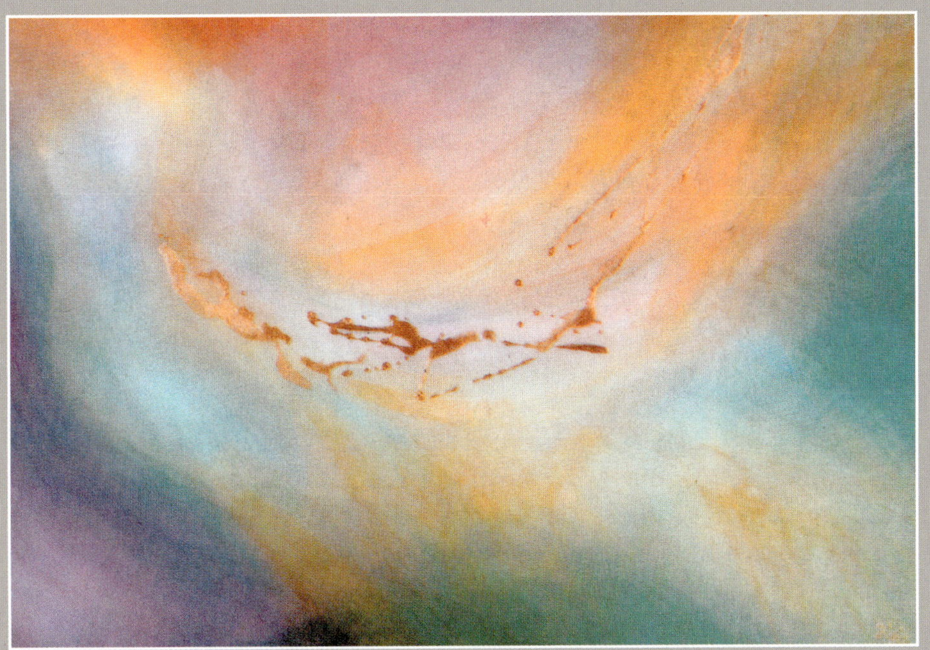

Angel

Taking us by the hand, this guide invites us to experience the different energies of the rainbow spectrum – allowing a shift of consciousness into higher levels of being with the promise of an integrated self.

Here the colours choose us and we are able to move freely across canvas, paper and other mediums. It is in this way that we can link into the thoughts, energies and emotions that wish to freely communicate themselves.

The emotional stream however deeply imbedded, is given permission to surface without criticism or judgment. It is in this way that negativity is released and transmuted, making space available for something new, healing, joyful, freeing and empowering.

Love and creativity are synonymous, both being born from a passionate involvement with the Beloved. Here the lover/artist interacts with the 'other' so that something new may be brought into being. This process is always a sensual one and subtle information and impressions are received from many channels.

We are all born naturally creative, and one of the primary reasons that we feel compelled to self-expression is that it links us into the universal stream of creative energy consciousness. What filters through, is dependant on what we have learnt to believe about not only ourselves, but also the world around us. It is here that our higher aspects participate, or more appropriately conspire as great alchemists to bring about a new creation or third force. This has a unique life of its own, and is capable of its own creative potential. Our creativity is a constant reminder that it is always up to us to take responsibility for all our thoughts and subsequent choices as they have the power to create positive or negative responses.

When we view health as essentially being a reflection of balance, it then follows that we can choose to determine the course of our own health by the way we live. The powers inherent within our bodies are such, that once we have acknowledged them and the ways in which they work we are more aware that we can actually use these same powers for our own healing.

By choosing to see ourselves as being greater than just our physical bodies, we are able to begin to recognize and accept that in truth we are cosmic beings of light, energy and colour. One might describe who we are as Radiant Rainbow Beings. Within us, each area and organ of the body can be identified by and associated with a particular colour that in turn has a specific frequency or vibration.

Because each colour constituant of light has its own vibratory wavelength with specific qualities of energy it is capable of affecting the whole gamut of human emotions allowing us to work with it therapeutically.

All physical matter may be described as being a 'spectral unity' with every part of our bodies resonating to specific colours.

We are bound to this ongoing creative relationship with life and always have the choice to experience this with either joy or difficulty thus allowing the experiential process to grow us beyond what we believe are our limitations.

Colour has had a major influence on every aspect of our lives since the dawn of time, and the more we understand our relationship with it the more we are able to incorporate and allow it to permeate and inform the way we live.

Everybody experiences colour differently because we all have our own inner responses to different colours. It is the way in which we relate to these, that describes at the deepest level who we are and what emotional stumbling blocks are still having a negative impact on our lives. It is a way to awakening and when combined with creativity, a deep response occurs, that can become a very effective tool for empowerment through releasing blockages.

This creative exploration, using colour, uncovers, layer by layer, those aspects of ourselves that are deeply buried in the unconscious, thereby affording a greater understanding and insight into our innate capacity to heal ourselves. Just by making the intention to work consciously with colour, we can initiate a whole process of self-discovery that can ultimately lead us where we want to go in life.

By allowing it, this spontaneous creative flow gives us the possibility of addressing disharmonies of the body, mind and spirit. We are automatically linked to our inner guidance system, which helps to free us of those rigid thinking patterns and paradigms that no longer serve our highest potential.

The nature of our creativity is to flow from what may be described as 'Space-less Space' and all it asks is that we are true to ourselves. When we allow that which wishes to emerge we can continue positively on our quest for wholeness and what lies beyond the veil of the visible. Within this relationship with what I term The Divine we are being continually asked to have faith as we surrender to a Greater Will.

Healing is quantum leaps of creativity

Deepak Chopra

Our inherent magnificence begs recognition and as we unfold and open to this possibility, we begin to fulfill our dreams and live our truth elegantly and positively.

By working with an emphasis on colour as the facilitator, the veil of memory is lifted as we express through colour those difficult experiences that have moulded us and often clouded our perceptions. These colour frequencies represent a language that reflects our inner responses to any given situation and by surrendering to this process we put ourselves in a position where we can bring ourselves back into our natural state of heightened awareness, into balance, restoring lost energy and re-empowering ourselves. We may then get to a place within which we are able to lovingly embrace all the potential that we have.

A tiny seed deep within moves and grows, spiralling ever upwards through the fabric of life. The roots seek nourishment from the deep remembrance that in essence we are re-aligning with the radiance of the Divine, and so the journey speaks of joy and pain, of celebration and colour, dreams and healing, peace and light, nature and texture. It speaks of love and wonder as it speaks through each of us, sounding the sound of 'creation'. It is the dance of life!

In Love and Light,

Fiona

COLOUR

A Soul Therapy

G-d is creating the entire universe fully and totally in this present now. Everything G-d created six thousand years ago – G-d creates now all at once...G-d is in everything, but G-d is nowhere as much as G-d is in the Soul...in the innermost and deepest aspect of the Soul – G-d creates the whole cosmos.

Meister Eckhart

When we see a rainbow, the invisible is momentarily made visible and our souls rejoice at being given a glimpse of a greater and different reality. We are reminded that it is only at the level of personality that we live in an illusion and where for the most part we are spiritually blind. This encounter with pure colour and light evokes great joy, because there is the remembrance and recognition of who we really are – Dancing, Cosmic Vibrations of Energy, Light and Colour.

From the beginning of time, rainbows have always held a certain fascination for mankind. They uplift and inspire and for many they remind us about the promise of ages that G-d made to Noah after the flood.

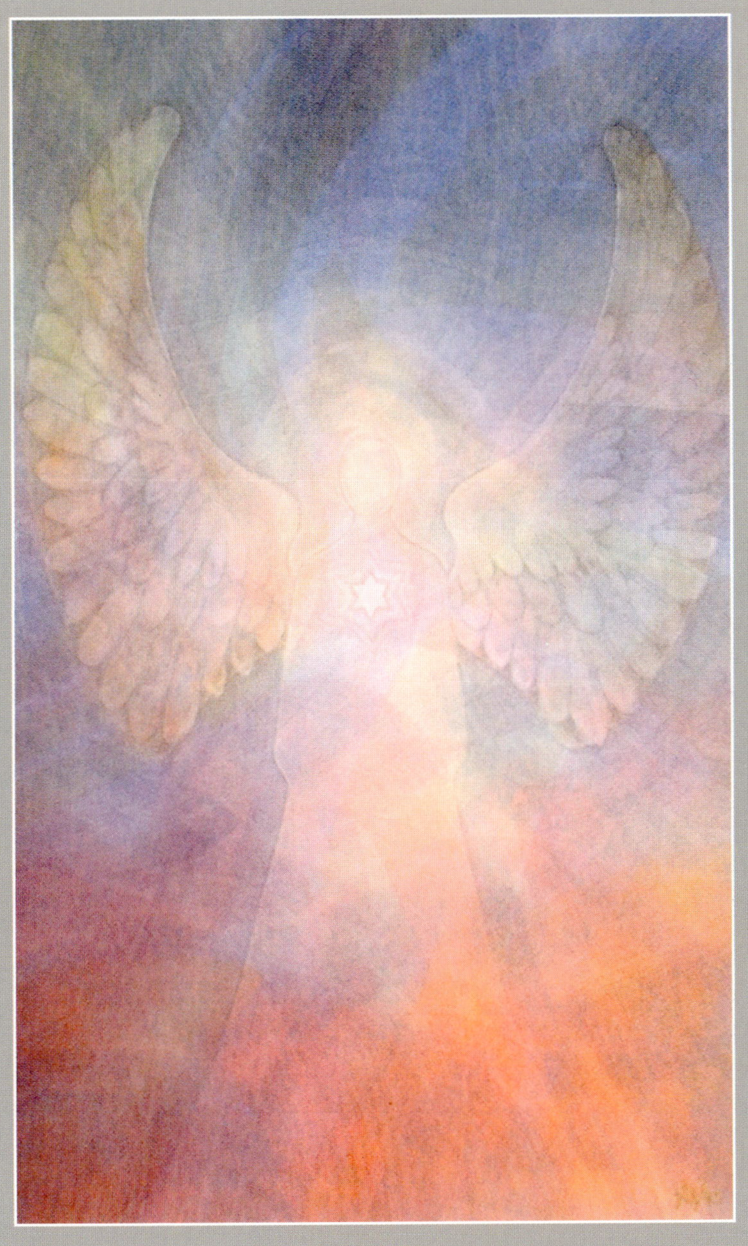

Higher Self
A symbol of inner and outer unification.

My bow I will put in the cloud and it will be a sign of the covenant between Me and the land, and when I bring clouds to the earth, the bow will be seen in the clouds, and I will remember My covenant between Me and you and between all living souls of all flesh.

In the book, 'Black Elk Speaks', Black Elk describes the passing through one door of perception to another. Here we are again reminded that when we are able to experience levels of a finer and subtler energy, the way the world appears changes and we are able to discern its multi-leveled nature according to our awareness.

Against the tree there was a man standing, with his arms held wide in front of him. I looked hard at him, but could not tell what people he came from. He was not a white man and he was not an Indian. While I was staring at him, his body began to change and became very beautiful with all colours of light and around him there was light.

As we come to accept more and more that we are colour vibrations and that these describe, define and express who we are, this leads us to work with the language of different frequencies for our own healing and empowerment.

We are Mind, Body and Spirit and every aspect of our being reflects the others. Since energy sustains all life, whenever there is an imbalance, one needs to look at the energy levels within particular areas. Like everything in life, Western medicine has positive and negative consequences.

On the whole it tends to accept a system of beliefs, which are more on a superficial level i.e. illness is seen to be a direct result of germs, viruses and microbes etc., which attack the body. These specific symptoms are then analyzed, observed and recorded. The name of the disease is attached to the symptoms and the therapy would often aims merely at alleviating the symptoms or outward manifestation of the illness. In theory therefore, we are healthy and it is those things mentioned that make us ill. In part this is accurate, but in essence, it is not a holistic view. Often times it is the curative measures that contribute to making us unwell, as they themselves are intrusive. This perception also separates us from nature's fundamental truths and many have become less aware of the dynamic inter-connectedness of all things, including the recognition that there are special relationships within the 'body'.

Nature nurtures the web of life.

Deepak Chopra

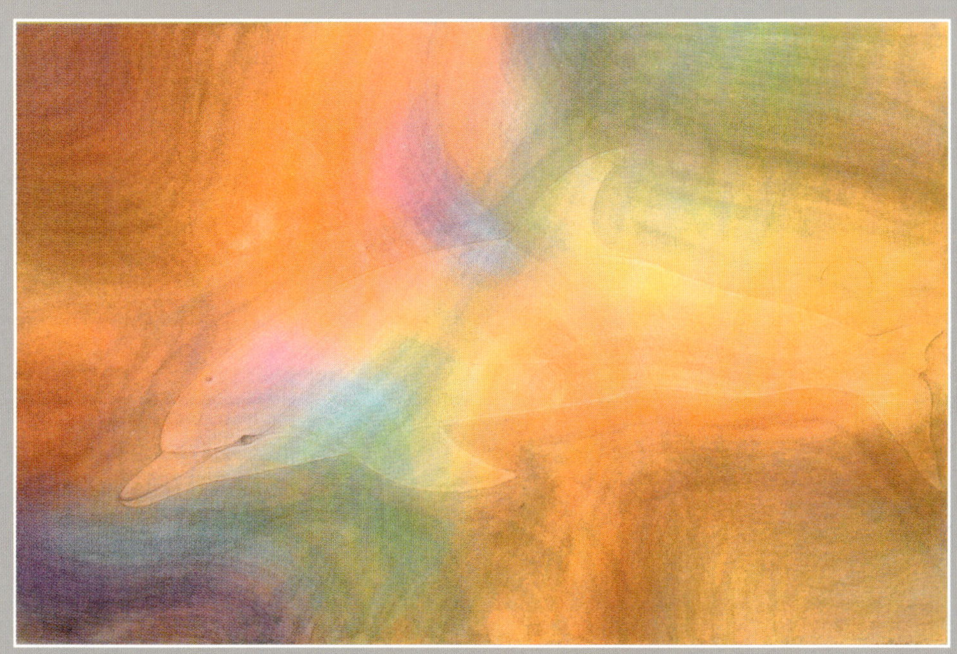

Into the Light

Inspiring us to care more committedly for the planet – reminding us of our stellar connections and evoking feelings of love and joy. These beings who live in the light, bless us with their presence and call us to celebrate in the moment.

A PERSONAL PROFILE

Ruthie's Invitation

All the world's a stage
And all the men and women merely players
They have their exits and their entrances
And one in his time plays many parts,
His acts being seven ages.

Shakespeare – As you like it

More than 27 years ago, a beautiful young woman named Ruthie whispered something to me that would change my life forever. Before quietly slipping out of this realm she gave me an invitation to 'Become the Best I could be'. Cleverly though, she made sure that this directive was received and heard at the deepest part of my being leaving me with only a sense of something very significant and a feeling of what those words would later come to imply.

At the time I conceded, partly because of the solemnity of the situation and partly because it was the first real moment of sense and peace in an otherwise emotionally fraught time. Having so easily agreed to this, I neither had the smallest inkling of what lay ahead nor the magnitude of the responsibility involved in honouring the agreement. What I didn't fully comprehend was that by learning what it meant to be the Best Me, I was not necessarily going to please everyone else. My ego was in for a trial by fire, especially the Good and Sweet aspects!

During that time in my life I was still dragging some of my teenage angst behind me and was desperately trying to make sense out of a situation that was obviously beyond me or my parents' control. They were faced with the loss of a daughter and I was faced with the loss of my only sister. We were living in a strange 'twilight-zone' and were not being counselled other than the occasional supportive word from the doctor or a relative. As a family we were limping through each day and lacking the appropriate skills for communicating our grief and anger. Of course there was a great deal of love but nothing of the psychological or emotional holding that we so desperately needed. Somewhere at the time I also believed it was my purpose to be there as a support and anchor for my heart-broken parents. If G-d had had to make a choice why hadn't he chosen me. Ruthie was young, vital, carefree and so giving of her love and compassion. I on the other hand was complex, introverted and socially ill-equipped. She had also been nursing the sick and dying and had remained with our parents. The burden of guilt and confusion was overwhelming.

So began my search for the answer to mankind's age old questions – Who am I? Why am I here? and What is my purpose?

At this time my body also began to show me the power of our thoughts. Before then I had never fully connected physical symptoms with an imbalance in the mind, body and spirit. Both my sister and mother were trained in the western medical way so it never occurred to me that by not working through this minefield of emotions was negatively impacting on me.

The result was that I erupted in boils. I was so terrified of losing control that my body in its wisdom took on the task of expressing what was so deeply held inside and I suppose one might say I started to 'boil' over! This caused me to cry, feel pain and release what I'd been so preciously guarding inside. My defences broke down and being vulnerable I was more easily able to connect with what was happening.

In the short while that followed Ruthie's passing, it also began to dawn on me that she had borrowed the key to my youth and left me to embark on a quest that was not only going to help me uncover many secrets about life, but also gain access through my own initiation schools to that which was sacred, mystical and sublime in life. I was to discover that 'Soul' spoke through me and as I really began to listen and pay attention I found that special Key to union with my G-d–Self. Truth was the name of this key and its treasure house was my Heart. As I began this journey into the miraculous I was to later understand that my beloved sister had elected to become my 'Guardian Angel'.

Even though the way forward at that time looked difficult and lonely, the energy of the magical was to start playing a much more significant role in my day-to-day living. It was as if the grief was allowing something new to emerge and this was demanding new expression. Everything that had been familiar and comfortable was being pulled from under me. Even my grief-stricken parents seemed to be part of the ploy and as co-conspirators they selflessly put me onto a flight into the 'deep end'.

Two things were very clear, one was that I now had the independence I had dreamed of and the other was that I was being faced with a head on collision with life. I was about to be confronted by all those situations that would so accurately mirror back my perceived view of the world. Was I in for a surprise!

My story is no more or less worthy than any other as I have and continue to experience all inner weathers, participating and evolving in the ever changing picture of my own thoughts and perceptions. Everyone who has ever touched my life forms an integral and significant part of it, each bringing their own unique colours. What has been shared is incorporated into a richly woven tapestry that grows and remains a 'Work in Progress'.

In writing this, I am endeavouring to meet with my Self more deeply and honestly and if in this process others feel invited and challenged to do the same, then glad my heart will be.

As ever, like the rest of us, I am bound to honouring those cycles of life that play themselves through every aspect of this 'Great Earth Walk'. The role players on the stage of my life theatre have been many and varied and my role in relation to each has revealed who I am. These aspects have at times been delightful and also sometimes frightening, but always wanting a voice. As I've looked into my heart I've looked into the Universal Heart, learning what it means to love and be loved. I have seen that accepting love as the source of all things helps one to become whole and that without love, the picture is like a broken mirror only reflecting distortion.

This Soul Quest that has had its focus on Light and Colour as the way to healing began in earnest at least fifteen years ago. During that time I had been living with the symptoms of ME or Chronic Fatigue Syndrome for several years. Even though I was working with healers, the turning point only came when I made the decision to heal myself by listening to my inner guidance. I was forced to face some very difficult facts about my life and needed to be more open and willing to embrace the darker aspects of who I was in order to become more authentic. I may have been given the possibility of starting a new life but I also took with me all the unresolved baggage from my past.

I recognised in myself the power of what one may call the 'Dark Mother' and the need we have to honour and express the wisdom that is held within her sacred womb. This particular part of my journey has at times been exacting and frightening. Not for the faint-hearted. It has called forth a deep respect and recognition of the workings of the subliminal and the process requires that one take full responsibility for everything that is hidden there.

Although I had been drawn to Psycho-Spiritual work from very early on, I found that some of it felt disparate. While parts of me were working well, I was not working as a unity. Somewhere I was crying out to reach and touch a greater joy and depth in my life. Again the key that I was presented with was that all I needed to do was to change the way I perceived life. My creativity was stunted and the arrow of self-doubt, shame and self-criticism had turned in on itself and was harming my very essence.

The themes of betrayal and loss brought me to the point in 1987 where I decided to face my own 'Blank Canvas'. I was 33 years old and decided that this was a good age to die to the old. Through meditation and visualization, I began letting go of my inner critic and started working instinctively and spontaneously on my first series of paintings. Initially I was tentative but kept returning to the place of my innocence and like a trusting child, began to engage with what I describe as the 'Spirit of Life'.

This life force came through in a very gentle and beautiful way, expressing itself in the palest of hues. It really felt as if I was being held and nurtured by a beneficent parent, who only wanted the best for me. This particular journey resulted one year later in the completion of 47 paintings which were exhibited at the Bristol Guild Gallery in England. So one might say that this has continued to be the way of my healing and the beginning of my love affair and exploration into the worlds of Light and Colour.

In particular the process of Veil – painting, has for me proven itself to be the doorway through which I have been able to venture into what may be described as other realms of reality. Here I've been given glimpses of life forms and energy patterns that have a different resonance to us. It has taught me to expect the unexpected and allow for the improbable.

The process of Veil - Painting may be likened to painting air. It involves applying hundreds of gossamer thin water-colour washes, which overlay each other allowing the light to shine through and the colour to remain pure. This ultimately has given definition to energy imprints.

On the whole the western mind wants to impose images and the process I'm sharing works in the reverse to this way of thinking because one waits to see what arises from the colour. It's a little like cloud watching. Often when we relax our gaze an image makes itself known. It involves total surrender to what I sense as a 'Higher Will'. I often ask the question of my students and clients,

How do we know what is there unless we keep opening to the possibility that there is always something more?

From my perspective, as we let go into the energy of love, our inner light illumines this world of higher resonance and we then have the possibility of transposing these images onto a material backdrop. To this day I do not plan or begin work with any definite image in mind of how it will be. I simply follow an inner directive, and like a dancer, move to the rhythm of an unseen drum. Linking creatively with life in this way, defies description. This is spontaneous, intuitive and has a profound influence on one's being. This communicates itself to the onlooker as well and we cannot go to 'sleep' again in the same way because there is a deep, soul recognition of what we have stood in front of. Here the experience one has with the process is what may be termed 'Existential' in the sense that there is no separation. Through intention, pure experience then exists beyond the level of energy. We simply become a part of All That Is.

This way of being has changed my life and my health has improved as I work realistically with my energy levels and keep building on those tools that help me return to my centre.

Creativity requires being totally present to what we are involved with. If one is passionate there is an engaging with the most fundamental part of our being, the part of us that exists as pure potentiality. This is creativity.

Even where there are atoms, and no elementary particles, and no protons, and no photons, suddenly elementary particles will emerge ...The base of the universe seethes with creativity, so much so that physicists refer to the universe's ground state as Space–Time Foam.

Scientist Brian Swimme

As a young girl, I remember finding my father sitting quietly in the garden. I asked him what he was doing, to which he replied with a smile, " Wu-Wei-ing". This in Zen Buddhist terms means doing without doing, effortless effort, without stress or struggle. It is the same when I am teaching or working therapeutically with another. I see my role as simply being open and available to that which needs to find expression. My preference has always been to facilitate others in this way thereby not imposing my will at any level.

Creativity is our birthright and everyone has something meaningful and unique to express. There is nothing more humbling, gratifying or joyful in my view, than watching as another is growing and healing through their own efforts and passion.

The image of the 'Blank Canvas' is one that I love. Like the beginner's mind, it is without past or future, devoid of rationality and emotionality.

It is without ego-identification, conditions or expectations. To put all of this aside and place oneself in front of the 'Blank Canvas' - to confront the void, can be daunting at first. But unless we turn and return to the empty space, that still centre, we are not free to move.

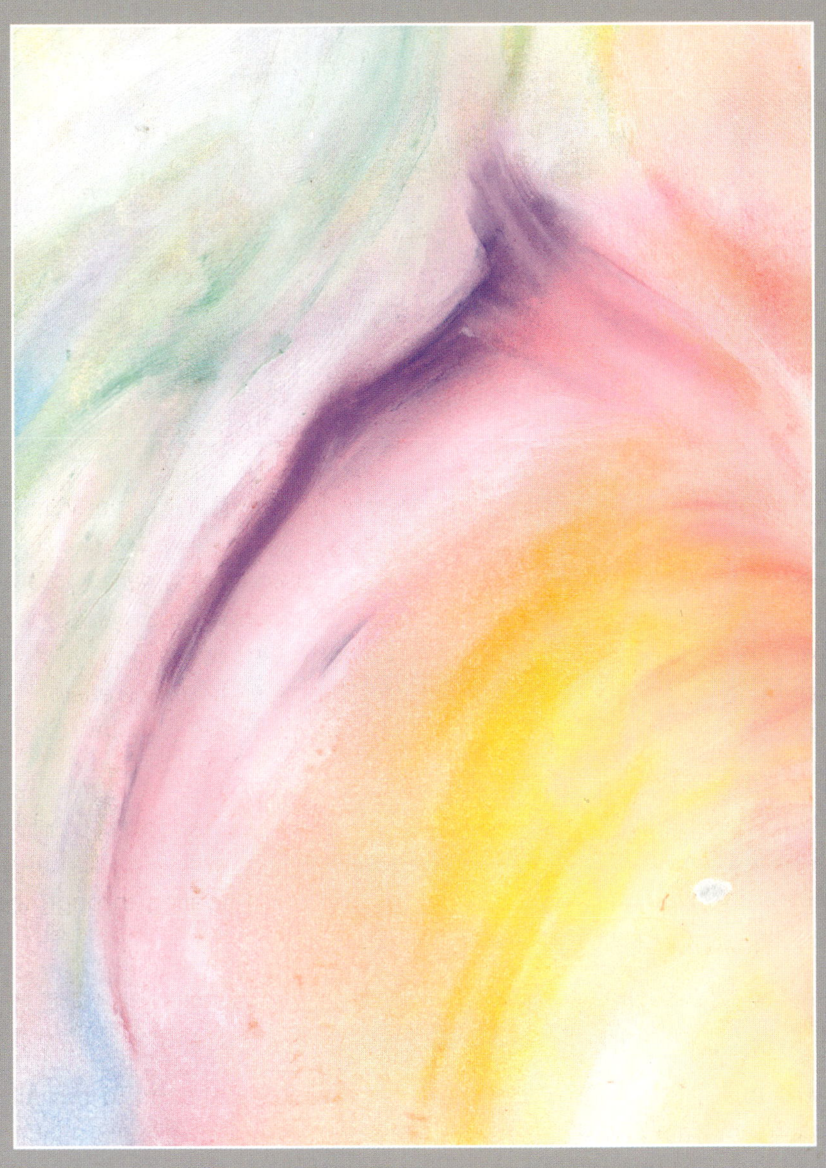

Jacob's Ladder

Healing Naturally

I believe that there was a time when all of us had auric sight. By this I mean that we had highly developed sensitivity to subtler levels of energy and colour. We were able to discern and see the colours around all living things and this ability enabled us to understand how everything in life interpenetrated and interacted with itself. We understood the language of colour and we used this knowledge with respect.

Over time, we have become desensitized and it is only a few who have retained this gift. This vision goes beyond the physical sense of sight and like children, we need to learn to re-own who we are as 'spiritual rainbow beings' in order to allow our natural abilities to re-surface.

We are all made up of energy. This energy has a frequency or vibrational quality, and the level of this defines all life. Energy can also be described in terms of specific fields and we ourselves are composed of overlapping fields of both higher and lower frequencies.

These frequencies, by their very nature have the potential to convey information, as well as being a system of filtration, discernment and perception. Because everything in life is composed of energy, and is in relationship to everything else, there is a constant flow of communication, and we, like the energy with which we are engaging, are always sending and receiving information at both the conscious and subliminal levels.

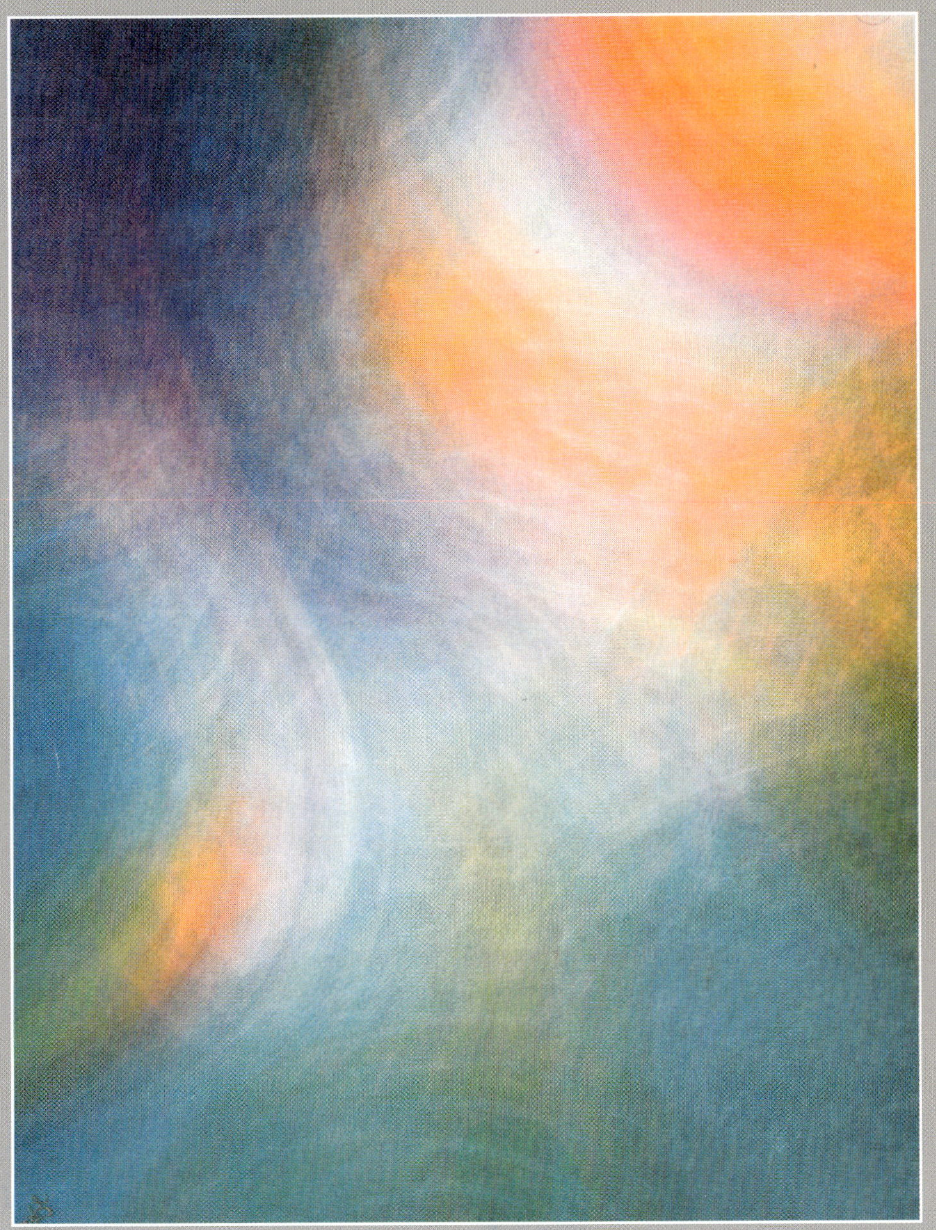

Rainbow

The secret of light held in the language of transcendent colour.

In many ways we may be likened to a 'computer' and it is our thoughts that create specific responses, which in turn are stored in our cells in what may be termed our 'cellular memory bank'.

If we take this further, and suggest that every thought impulse has a frequency and that frequency may be seen as a colour, imagine the incredible colour story we each have. From a subtle, anatomical viewpoint, colour may be seen as working directly through specific subtle energy centres known as chakras.

Each chakra has its own particular function and purpose and as we master the lessons associated with these energy centres we grow spiritually, gaining Self-power and knowledge. We see more and more that we are made of light, and this moves us along the path of enlightenment.

From a Hindu perspective, our energy system may be likened to a vertical column that has three main channels of energy which come together at specific junctures. These channels, or streams are known as Ida, Pingala and Shushumna. It is at the point where they intersect that the 'chakras' or 'energy wheels' are located. These are the 'very core' of the aura and in order to ensure that the energies flow in harmony, each chakra should be fully open and in balance. They are each identified by colour and these colours in turn act as the keys to our healing. By introducing the appropriate colour, the weakened wavelength of energy is reinforced and balance re-established.

The higher and subtler cosmic energies are taken in by the chakras, where they are transmuted into a more utilizable form within the physical body.

In other words the chakras act as transformers and the higher cosmic energy is stepped down to a lower level. When this takes place, it is then translated into hormonal, physiological and eventually cellular changes throughout the body.

There are both major and minor chakras and each of the seven major chakras is associated with a major nerve plexus and endocrine gland. In working with the chakra system, one may describe them sequentially as the first chakra, which is positioned at the base of the spine, to the 7th chakra which is at the top of the crown.

The energy of our life force flows into our bodies from the top of our heads and nourishes and energises each chakra as it moves down through the length of the spinal column. From an Eastern tradition, this cosmic energy is known as the 'Breath of Life' or 'Prana'.

In order to more fully understand who we are and how our energy systems work in the bigger picture, we need to move away from the belief that we are just what we see.

Our higher energy systems are directly connected to and working with the material or physical body. These are made up of matter which has a different nature to the physical, but even so they are able to occupy the same space. One may refer to these lower subtle bodies as the 'physical aura' and they are defined by what they do, their radiance and where they are located. These layers, like the physical have an identifiable structure but in addition possess extra forms.

If one looks at the chakras, one sees that they resemble funnels, with the narrow pointed end facing into the main vertical column of energy and it is their open, wider ends that extend to the edge of each layer of the energy field they are located in.

This first layer, which extends slightly beyond the physical body, is referred to as the 'Etheric Body'. This is responsible for cellular guidance and the physical cannot survive without it. If there is distortion of any kind in the Etheric, physical disease soon follows. It acts like a template for the body and appears as a fine whitish blue radiance surrounding the physical.

In addition to the Etheric, there are many bodies of even higher and subtler composition.

The next is the 'Emotional Body' and unlike the Etheric, it does not duplicate the physical in that it is much more fluid and appears as moving, changing clouds of different colours. It is involved with feelings and the expression of emotions.

The Mental Body is the next field of visible energy and it is through this that the self manifests and expresses the concrete intellect. The energy of the mental realm has its effect upon the physical by initially being processed through the other subtle bodies. This field appears as a bright yellow radiance around the head and shoulder area, and may also extend around the whole body.

These first three layers, including the physical body, form what is termed the 'physical aura'. Everything that we have ever experienced is integrated at the higher levels of vibration.

This includes all that we've ever learnt and understood in every past lifetime, because, unlike the 'physical aura' or lower bodies, the higher ones have permanence.

Our 'true aura' is produced at this higher level. It has a transcendental brilliance and colour that acts as our guidance system and describes our soul's purpose and intention.

NB: [This subject is dealt with in greater depth in the chapter - Heaven Knows]

A RAINBOW LADDER TO THE STARS

A brief description of the Chakras, their colours and relationship to the Endocrine System

The following information on the Chakras may help one to better understand the workings of the body and mind in terms of blockaging or dysfunction resulting from situations that have negatively impacted one's life and have not been fully addressed or resolved.

If we make the analogy between our Chakra system and a ladder, then every rung of 'our' rainbow ladder has a specific colour which works in direct relation to the next. As an ascending scale of colour, we begin with the first rung, which represents our closest connection to the earth.

The Endocrine system helps the nervous system regulate various bodily activities. The glands included in this system have no ducts and the secretions or hormones from them pass directly into the blood- stream and have a widespread effect throughout the body.

Universal Key

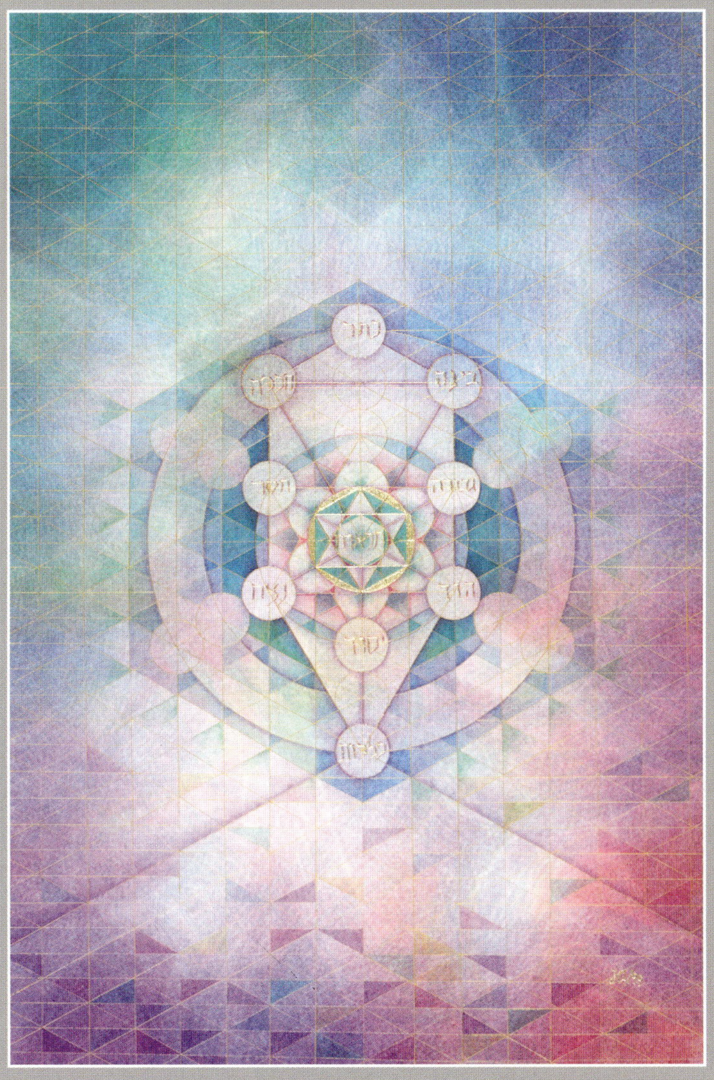

Tree of Life

The symbol of 'Oneness' the 'Tree of Ascension' held in the light of G-d's love - each step offering us new life, new vision.

1st - Base or Root Chakra

This chakra relates to our primal and instinctual nature. Depicted by the colour red and known as the root or base chakra,which is located at the base of the spine and is defined as the chakra that governs understanding of the physical world. This chakra is linked to the Adrenal Glands of our Endocrine system and governs the Kidneys and Spinal column.

The Adrenal Glands, which are governed by the first chakra, are situated just above the Pancreas. Their physical function is that of regulating the metabolism; in other words, the process by which the body turns food into energy and living tissue. It helps the body adjust to stress as well as increasing the amount of sugar in the blood. In addition to this, it increases the heart rate and blood pressure.

When we look at the function of these glands, it gives us an understanding of how they relate to the other organs - for example, in a stressful situation such as exercise, cold, injury, suffocation or any other situation causing fear, anxiety, pain, fall in blood pressure or blood sugar, there is a flood of nervous impulses to the hypothalamus. This nervous stimulation, via the sympathetic nerves, causes the adrenalin and noradrenalin to be released into the blood system. These hormones then act on tissue throughout the body and their overall effect is to prepare the body for aggressive activity and exertion by diverting the blood to the limb muscles, increasing the action of the heart, dilating the bronchial tubes, mobilizing liver glycogen to raise blood sugar and reducing most other activity, for example in the gut. We call this a flight or fight action. It is here where we learn to understand our interconnectedness and interrelationship with all life, the first lessons being the trusting and nurturing in a family context. This then would follow through to community, and ultimately to all life.

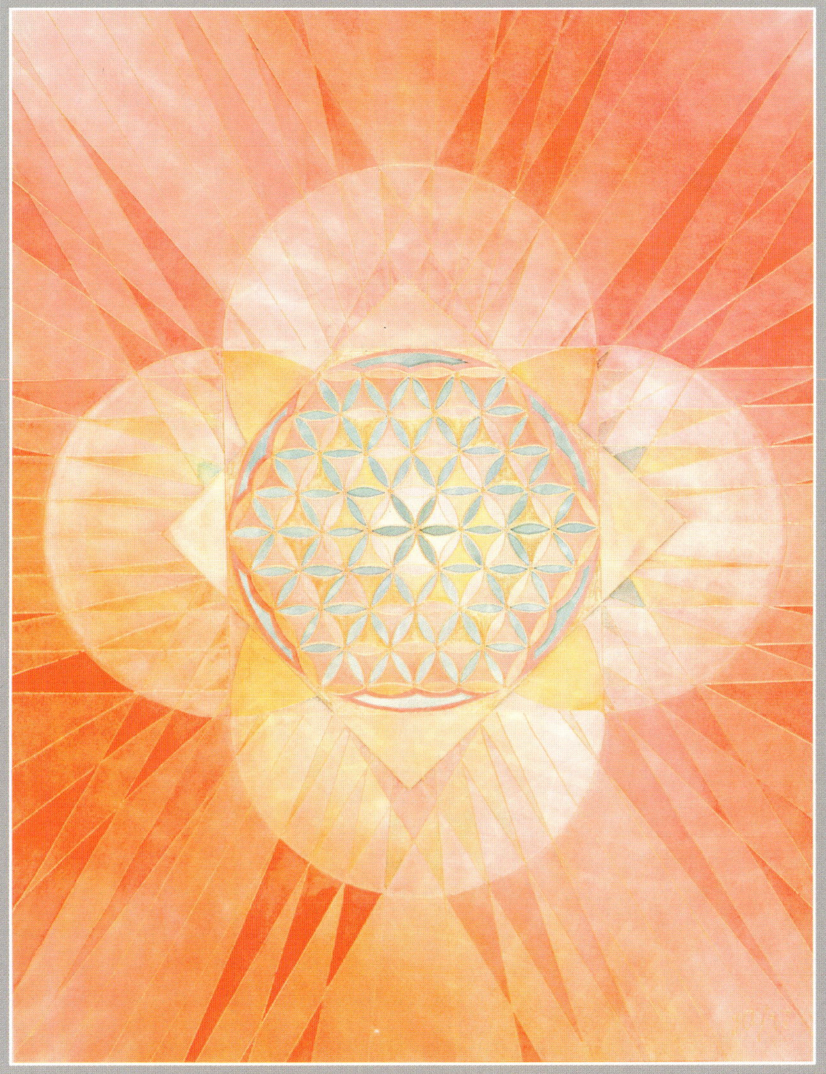

Sunburst

This is the part of us that relates directly to our need to procreate, survive and feel secure or rooted and supported by life. When we are unable to engage fully with life at this level, for whatever reason, we do not feel safe or grounded. We feel unsupported by the world around us and many times the particular dysfunctions occur as a result. These can include all problems related to our lower vertebral column, the ureters, the kidneys and adrenal gland functions ie; chronic lower back pain, sciatica, varicose veins, rectal difficulties and in extreme cases, cancer.

When there is balance and harmony in this area we are more fully able to engage with the positive qualities. These include feeling grounded, having a sense of belonging as well as a determination to succeed in life. We feel that we can be independent and that our courage and perseverance will see us through. Red is also a colour of passion symbolizing the Spirit of Life (in the physical)

2nd - or Sacral Chakra

This chakra is located approximately two finger-breadths below the navel and is associated with the colour orange. It's the second 'rung' up the ladder and is associated with the reproductive glands, the Ovaries in women and Testes in men. It governs our attitudes in relationships, particularly with regard to money, sex and the way we are influenced and affected by power and control. In our growth process it is related to the way we interact, specifically the way in which we treat, respect and honour others and vice versa.

When there is difficulty in the normal flow of energy here, it may manifest as problems related to the sexual organs, lower intestine, lower vertebrae, pelvis, appendix and bladder.

At the physical level, in relation to the endocrine system, the secretion from the ovaries stimulates development of the female sexual organs and sexual characteristics. It stimulates female sexual behaviour and regulates menstruation. It also causes the birth canal to widen. Like the ovaries, the secretion of the Testes stimulates the development of male sex organs, sexual characteristics and sexual behaviour.

Orange, in this context may be associated with the qualities of creativity, aspiration, inspiration, renunciation, increased awareness of other people's needs, self-knowledge, mindfulness, courage, deep joy, bliss and dedication. It is also related to deep trauma, shock and sexuality in its expressive form. In relationship it is about dependency and co-dependent issues.

3rd - or Solar Plexus Chakra

The third or Solar Plexus Chakra is located in the Solar Plexus region, just above the navel. It is linked to the pancreas and governs the workings of the liver, spleen, stomach, gall bladder and certain aspects of the nervous system. This third 'rung' of the ladder, is associated with the colour yellow and it is here that we process and filter emotional issues, particularly around our personal power. We learn as we grow to honour ourselves and to listen to what our 'gut' or instinctual natures tell us about people, places and situations.

Here is the seat of our survival intuition and when it is functioning well, we are able to discern and filter out those things that may harm us. In other words we become aware of the negative energies, particularly physical danger. It is here that we receive our first impressions. This is the prana assimilator of the soul and is referred to as our Central Sun. In this growth process we learn to have self-worth and self-esteem. So if there is damage in this area we need to look at where our energy or power is going and also how we digest life. Are we easily intimidated and do we feel rejected, what are our interpersonal - relationship skills like and do we take responsibility for the choices we make? All these questions are directly related to the functioning of this chakra.

This part of the body is where we digest life. In this region, the Pancreas is the Endocrine gland that is governed by the Solar Plexus chakra. It secretes a powerful digestive juice into the gut and is positioned just below the Adrenal glands.

Within the Pancreas are tiny clumps of cells known as the Islets of Langerhaans and within these are two types of cells -

1. Alpha cells which secrete glycogen.
2. Beta cells which secrete the protein insulin at a rate which increases with the rising levels of glucose in the blood.

Glucagon increases blood sugar levels by mobilizing glycogen from the liver. It also mobilizes stored fat and causes the rapid release of insulin from the islets.

Insulin is essential to life. Its fundamental effect is to increase the transport of glucose into cells. It also increases protein synthesis in all cells as well as the laying down of fat in adipose tissue. It is necessary for the full breakdown of fatty acids by the liver.

If we now look at this from a growth perspective, the issues related to the dysfunctioning of the Solar Plexus chakra could result in problems with the gall bladder, arthritis, indigestion, pancreatitis, diabetes, cancer of the pancreas, flu, nausea and the eating disorders anorexia and bulimia.

4th - or Heart Chakra

This chakra is the fourth 'rung' up our developmental ladder and is associated with the colour green. The endocrine gland that is governed by this centre is the Thymus Gland. The Heart Chakra is found at the sternum in the centre of the chest. If we look at the colour green, it is the centre of the colour spectrum and contains the yellow of the lower magnetic colours and blue of the higher electric colours. It is the pivotal centre of balance and the lessons related to it are all aspects to do with love, forgiveness and compassion.

When we are functioning well at this level, we are able to create from the heart and follow our heart's desire. We also learn to love and respect all other life forms. Here we learn, as we grow, to give and receive love, and in doing so we are able to open to 'love as a divine power'.

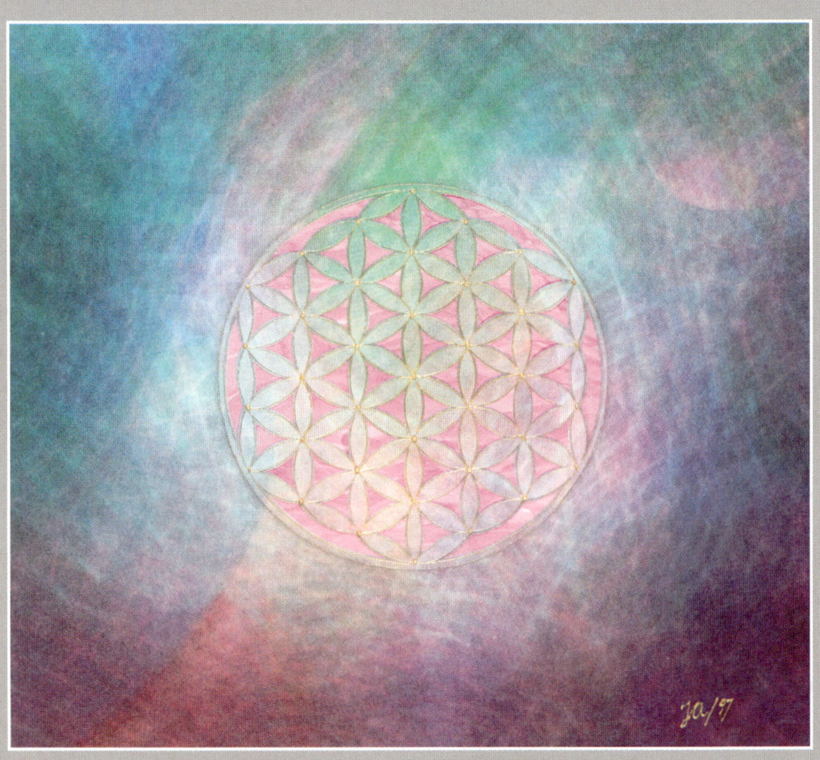

Seed

The areas governed by this chakra other than the heart, are the lungs and circulatory system. The physical problems that may arise in relation to an imbalance in this area might include heart conditions, asthma, allergies, lung problems, circulation problems and upper back and shoulder problems.

5th - or Throat Chakra

This chakra is known as the Throat Chakra and it governs the Thyroid and Parathyroid glands. It is associated with the colour blue and is connected to all issues regarding self-expression and personal will. It is the fifth 'rung' up the rainbow ladder and acts as a bridge to the unseen worlds other than the physical.

The Thyroid and Parathyroid govern the lungs, vocal cords, bronchial apparatus and the metabolism. This centre at a personal development level is concerned with communication, expression and correct judgement.

At a physical level the function of the Thyroid increases the rate of metabolism and also decreases the amount of calcium in the blood. The Parathyroid increases the amount of calcium in the blood as well as decreasing the amount of phosphate.

The imbalances in these areas can manifest in the larynx, trachea, esophagus, neck vertebrae, mouth, teeth gums and jaw.

Dysfunctions can include raspy throats, all throat problems, mouth problems, jaw misalignment, scoliosis, stiff neck, laryngitis, tonsillitis, thyroid problems and headaches.

When there is balance and harmony in this area we are able to express ourselves confidently, clearly and with a sense of purpose. We feel connected to a higher will as opposed to our ego-based will and take responsibility for the impact that the spoken word can have.

Blue can also be helpful for under and overactive thyroid, speech impediments, tension, infections, bruising, labour and teething in babies.

Blue like the other colours has many aspects to it but essentially it can be calming and pacifying. It may be beneficial in the reduction of the overproduction of cancerous cells and can also help to bring relief in relationship problems where one needs to express difficult feelings and assist where one is making a transition as well as in clairvoyance and channelling.

6th - or Third Eye Chakra

The Pituitary gland is governed by the Third Eye chakra and is associated with the colour indigo. The organs associated with this gland are the brain, eyes, ears, nose and Pineal gland. It may be said that this is notably one of the most important of the endocrine glands. At the personal development level it is associated with the use of knowledge, reasoning and intuitive skills.

Universal Key

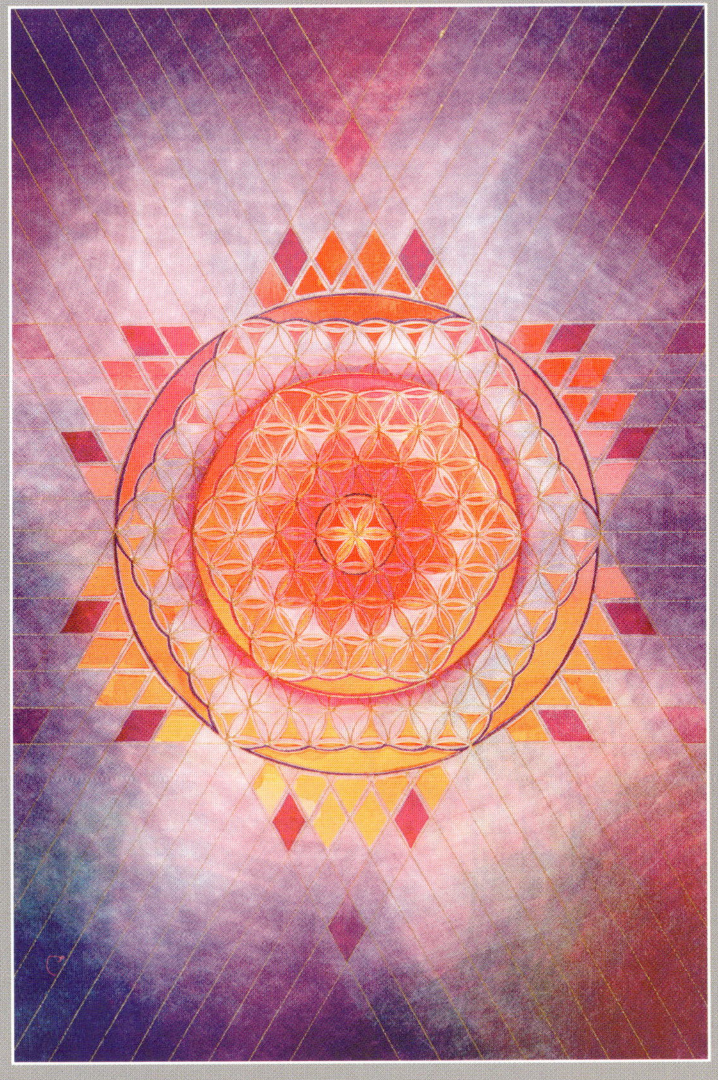

Midnight Star

When this chakra is functioning well we learn to think and reason based on higher meaning and purpose.

Physically, this gland consists of two parts, the anterior and posterior lobes. The former releases hormones that regulate the secretions of many other endocrine glands and for this reason it is sometimes known as the Master Gland. The secretions of the anterior lobe stimulate production of various hormones by the adrenal cortex. It stimulates the growth of ovarian follicles in females and seminiferous - tubules in males. It promotes the secretion of thyroxine by the thyroid gland, the production of milk by the mammary glands, and general body growth.

The function of the posterior lobe of the Pituitary gland stimulates the muscles of the uterus to contract during labour. Finally it stimulates the kidneys to retain water as well as causing the blood vessels to contract. Common imbalances in these areas may include brain problems, neurological disorders, blindness, deafness, epilepsy, full spinal difficulties, migraine and tension headaches, comas, depression and addiction.

The main theme of the colour indigo, is about helping us to understand that life is essentially spiritual. When used therapeutically this colour can be calmative as well as a stimulant in the process of bringing to the fore old memories where one needs to let go of old belief systems and patterns.

The deep magenta within the indigo also helps to connect with one's higher purpose. Indigo is useful for balancing the emotions and overcoming feelings of separation and can be empowering when working with issues of self – love.

Universal Key

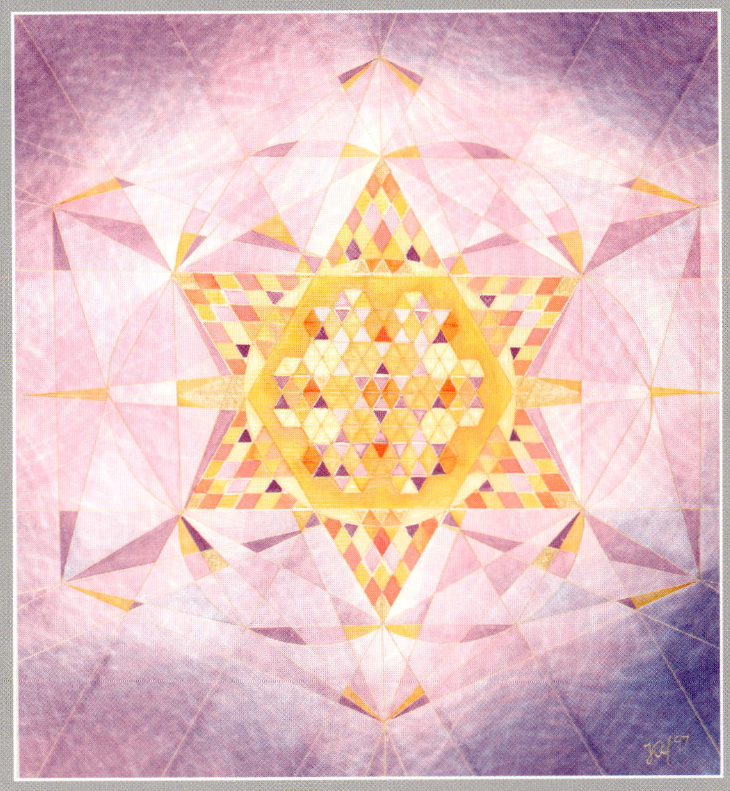

Golden Star

At a physical level it is helpful with bruises, grazes, all pain, bronchitis, high blood pressure, cystitis, diarrhoea and sciatica.

Spiritually this sixth chakra is especially important in the area of intuition and dreaming.

7th — or Crown Chakra

This chakra governs the Pineal Gland and is associated with the colour violet. The function of the gland is to secrete various chemical substances such as melatonin. It is recognized sometimes as a light-sensing organ and as a biological clock. It is a ductless gland and the secretions regulate the activity of sex glands. The specific areas that are under its influence include the nervous system, the skin and skeletal structure, the right eye and upper brain. When there is an imbalance in these areas dysfunctions may include nervous disorders, paralysis, genetic disorders, bone problems and multiple sclerosis.

It is at this level that we learn and absorb through discernment, our attitudes, values and ethics in life. When it's functioning well, we are able to fully accept our lives and our capacity to fulfill our life purpose.

As a colour, violet can be beneficial in calming erratic emotions and internal and external inflammation. It is also good for subduing heart palpitations, cases of concussion, jangled nerves and supporting the immune system.

NB: It is important to understand that one need direction from a qualified colour practitioner when it comes to using colour for specfic and serious conditions. There are obviously times when following one's instinct is absolutely appropriate, but as we are all different so are our needs and the choice of colour must be made on an individual basis.

Universal Key

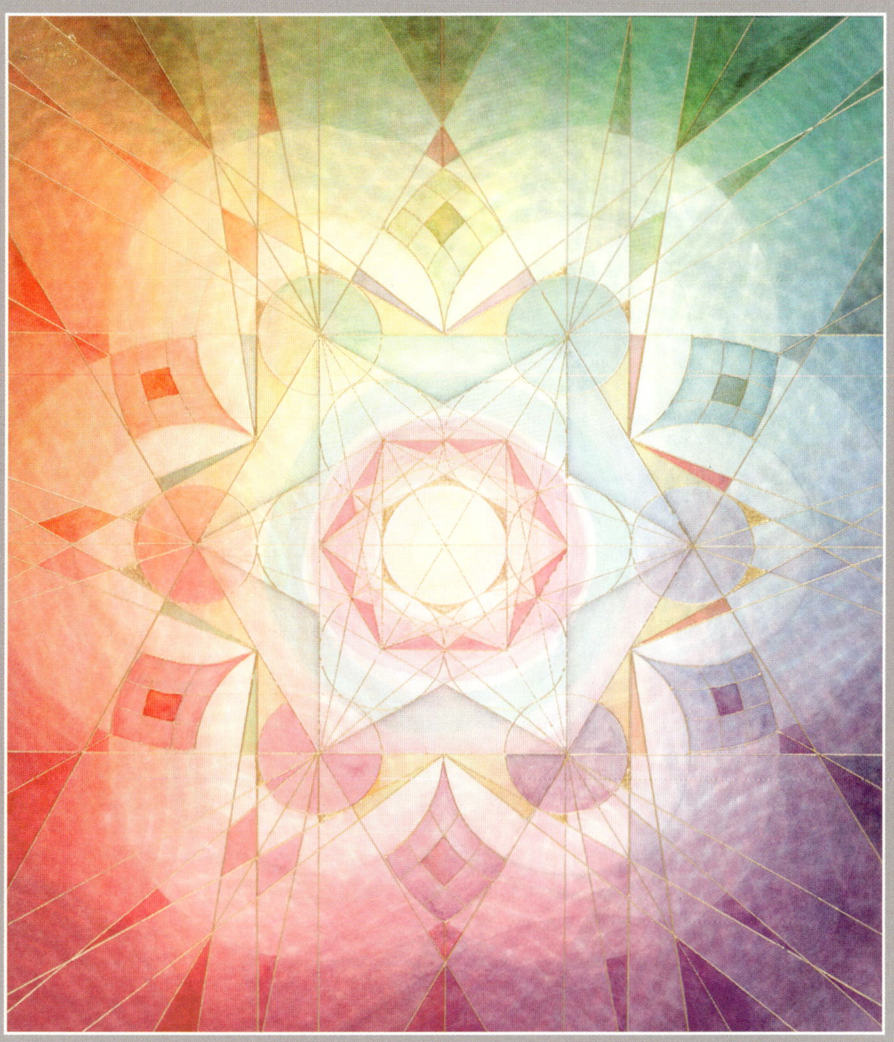

Kaleidoscope

HEAVEN KNOWS

The Power of Colour to Heal Us

G-d's Word is in all Creation, visible and invisible.
The Word is living, being, spirit, all verdant and greening, all creativity...
This Word manifests in every creature... Now this is how the spirit is in the flesh – the Word is indivisble from G-d

Hildegard of Bingen

To write about the way in which colour actually acts to heal the physical and subtle bodies is to enter into an area of knowledge that we as a race are just beginning to remember from a time long ago. We are learning once more to own the fact that as intelligence we 'orchestrate' energy.

As we consider ourselves multi-dimensional beings in nature we see that we too are part of a multi-dimensional world. All that exists on this planet is stepped down vibrational energy and everything that we need at every level is also part of what there is.

A simple example of this is the patient in hospital. It is customary to give flowers or fruit as a gift. In truth what we are doing is giving what we sense and believe to be healing. This is a gesture of great wisdom as each of the fruits or flowers has its own specific colour vibration and qualities. The patient will naturally take in those energies and in turn these will feed a particular need in certain areas.

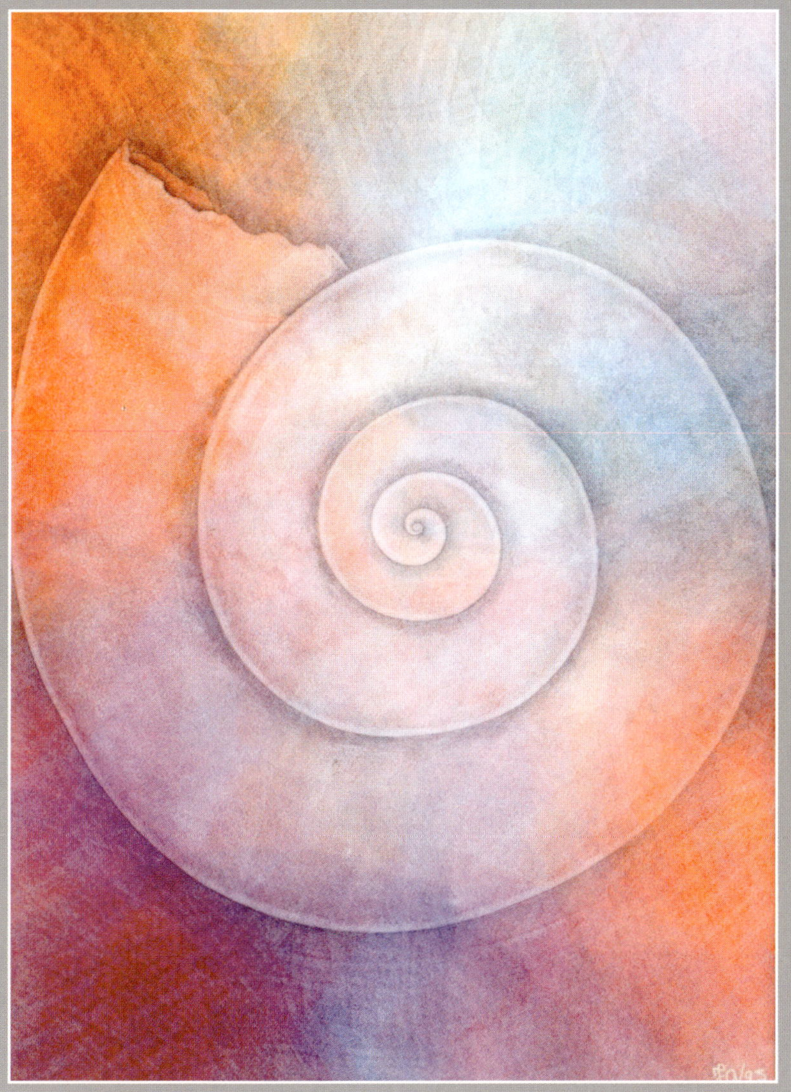

The Colour of Love

Rainbow translucence spiralling through all nature reflecting the universe in a shell.

For example pink carnations or roses may well evoke a renewed sense of a connection to love and acceptance in the face of pain, difficulty and the sense of loneliness. Golden chrysanthemums would be uplifting and evoke a sense of joy. All of these things help to bring the colour back into our lives especially at times of loss, injury and damage to ourselves through negative patterning. They help to get us back on track.

From an esoteric perspective, colour is the direct result of the vibration of light. As the colour is increased in speed it becomes more vibrant and more brilliant. It is said that as light descends it does so in a circular way and that it is initially projected from a specific point quite spontaneously. In other words this source of light is an intense white and as it expands in circumference there is a progressive slowing down and in the process a taking on of colour. The premise is then that the radiation or light is released according to a specific objective. This implies that light has purpose and that there is a greater power and intelligence directing its projection.

When we understand at a conscious level the significance of the specific energy of each colour, we are then in a position to relate this to our divinity. In time our consciousness begins to expand, allowing the unique qualities to inspire, inform and move us beyond the limitations of the physical world.

Mankind has the potential for finding a great peace and harmony but in order to do this it will be necessary to raise our entire awareness so that we can hold the amount of light that will make this possible. Only then when we have aligned ourselves with our greater purpose can we all move forward and actually live our dream of freedom from fear.

Our choices will be made from a purity of intent for the greater good and our motivation will come from a place of purity and deep connection to the divine within each of us.

At this time the majority of humanity relates to seven major rays of the rainbow spectrum, each of which at the highest level represents a particular quality of being. These are – love, wisdom, faith, peace, purity, justice and freedom.

Man's spirit and soul is composed of light. All matter may be seen as 'frozen light'. It has recently been proven scientifically at the Institute of Biophysics in Kaiserlauten, Germany that the cells of all living things in nature radiate light. This is represented by a regulating field of energy that encompasses the whole organism and exerts a vital influence on all bio-chemical processes within the body. This inter-cellular communication is in essence cellular intelligence.

In trying to understand more fully what our relationship is to the different colour vibrations I have needed to go on a very revealing, honest and often exciting journey. One that has required I explore many texts as well as using my own experience through clairvoyance and sensing colour. In the next few paragraphs I aim to share in the simplest and clearest way my understanding of energy as expressed through colour. The following feels like the most appropriate description at a Soul level for me.

Imagine that as Soul we make a conscious decision to experience life in physical form and in this instance, as a Human Being. At Soul level we exist as Light and this presents as a great colour radiance that is unique to us as Soul.

All the other Soul Energies at the different levels also have their own special and defining colours. As mentioned previously these colours all carry with them purpose and specific qualities of being and are projected for a particular reason.

When we incarnate we bring these colours with us into the world of matter so that they will act as a guidance system to express our Soul's purpose for the specific lifetime. We may refer to this combination of colours as our Soul Print and unlike the physical aura this is what may be termed the Soul's True Aura. It is this True Aura that links us to the Higher Consciousness of All Being which in turn continues its journey through eternity.

This True Aura can identify the Soul essence and it holds the record of the Soul in many ways like fingerprints can be used to identify an individual. Whatever has been experienced from the beginning of time has left its mark upon this Aura. The main difference between the two types of aura are that the Physical Aura and its colours relate to the Chakras or Energy Wheels, whose function is to determine and regulate physical health and balance. This body is not eternal and when it dies, the Life force with its colours transmute.

Having had previous incarnations, each Soul would select a main purpose, and this would be amplified and carried for the length of one's life through one coloured ray, with one or more supplemental rays next to it.

While you were living in the higher dimensions there was a thorough examination of your Soul Record; all you had experienced and learned to that point. [We can't really define it as time here because time does not exist at this level.]

This assessment by teachers and guides would constitute a kind of evaluation. So before you came to the planet you knew, in essence the reason for doing so. You would not return without great clarity and without the Soul capacity of magnificence and commitment. The one thing that would be yours at every point would be the fact that you had free will. So even if you were given all the support in the world every thing would come down to the choices you made in relation to the situations you set up. The people you would act alongside on your theatre of life stage, would have made a prior Soul contract for specific reasons. These people could even be from the same Soul Group as yourself.

Acting on the advice, that you would be given guides and teachers and a primary colour of intention with its supplemental rays to help you complete your task, you made the decision to be reborn.

The chest area contains a blaze of brilliantly coloured light that continues streaming for the duration of the physical life. This conveys the Soul's messages reminding you of the reason for rebirth and what the soul had hoped to accomplish. You would be drawn to those specific interests and activities that would most greatly benefit your purpose. As soon as you entered Earth's vibrational field you would need to go through a process of forgetting. At the level of personality you would experience this as if being blindfolded and taken to an unfamiliar place.

These Soul Colours radiate vertically into the Earth's gravitational pull so that you are attached, to the Earth. They also extend to approximately three feet above your head and because the Great Rays descend in a way that is comparable with rainfall, your Personal Rays extend above your head and are in turn easily nourished by them.

This brings us now to the point where it is important to understand that at this time we are receiving at a spiritual level, vibrations that are being sent by the Great Lords Of Light. These Beings have transcended earthly limitations and are working with humanity to serve a higher purpose through their guidance, compassion and unconditional love. They are helpers of the very highest order. In particular, they are, through their teaching, encouraging us to understand the ways in which Universal law works through our lives; so that when we are able to fully acknowledge its potential and limitless power we can consciously use this energy to create miracles.

Our first step requires that we learn to detach ourselves from the negative, collective unconscious with its belief structures. This involves processing and clearing at the deepest level and learning to act with absolute integrity from our highest source of truth.

These patterns are imprinted at a cellular level because we need this loving guidance system to support us in order to facilitate our healing process. It is through each Master of Light that we have access to the whole Spectrum of Masters; each one being a specialist in their own field.

Each colour that is visible with the naked eye not only has its own qualities and purpose, but also a particular Master who is assigned to it and is responsible for its power. Often in our lifetimes one particular Master will be drawn to overseeing and guiding us.

When we do not acknowledge and listen to the guidance of our True Self as opposed to our Personality, this literally discolours our energy bodies and our lives.

Whatever prevents us from living our truth has a negative impact and results in a 'sick aura'. This is nearly always the reason we become ill. So in essence if we learn to treat and understand ourselves at this Auric level we will be able to correct any disturbance whether at a physical, mental or spiritual level.

We are, a multi-dimensional cohesion of energy fields, interdependent and interfacing, integrated into a miraculous, individual oneness, reflecting the greater whole. Everything, from conscious thought to cellular process, is an electromagnetic oscillation, a degree of frequency vibration, a bio-manifestation of the one primal energy of light.

David Bohm

Qualities of The Visible Spectrum

The following description of the colours is a short guide to their particular properties and recognizable qualities and is not meant as a comprehensive description of all the different subtleties of the hues and tones.

Red

When we look at this colour in relation to the first chakra and our physical body, we can associate it with alignment to feelings of connectedness to the Earth and the inner strength that comes from feeling part of and secure in the physical world. As we grow and develop in a healthy environment we feel powerful, confident, supported and are able to manifest our plans and dreams as well as being able to lay down strong roots. We feel nurtured and vital. In other words we have a true passion for life and are well grounded. We see and experience the interconnectedness of all life and believe in ourselves.

Red can also help to encourage one to find one's passion by re-directing energy away from activities based on fear. If one freely associates about this colour, it soon becomes obvious that there are some generally accepted ideas that we share. Like everything in our world there are always two sides or polarities to everything. We live with duality, so just as there are positive attributes of each colour there are also negative ones; in other words a light and dark side.

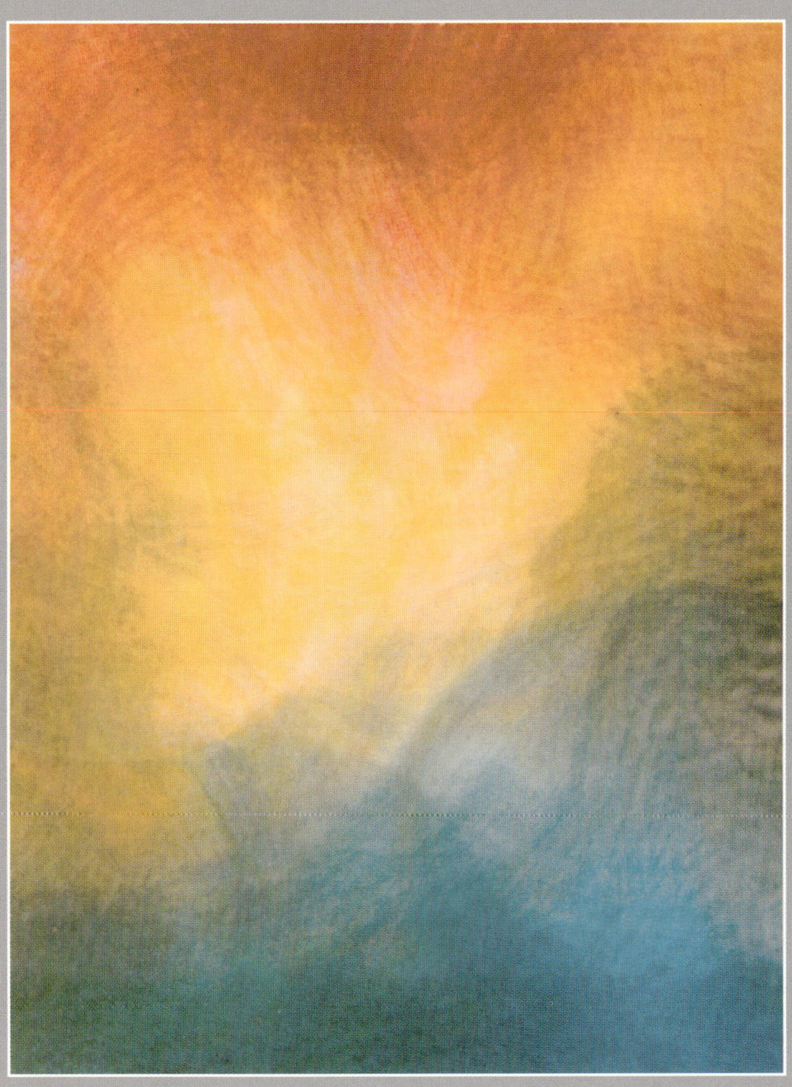

Shore
A balancing of the energies of heaven and earth – the perpetual flow of spirit in matter

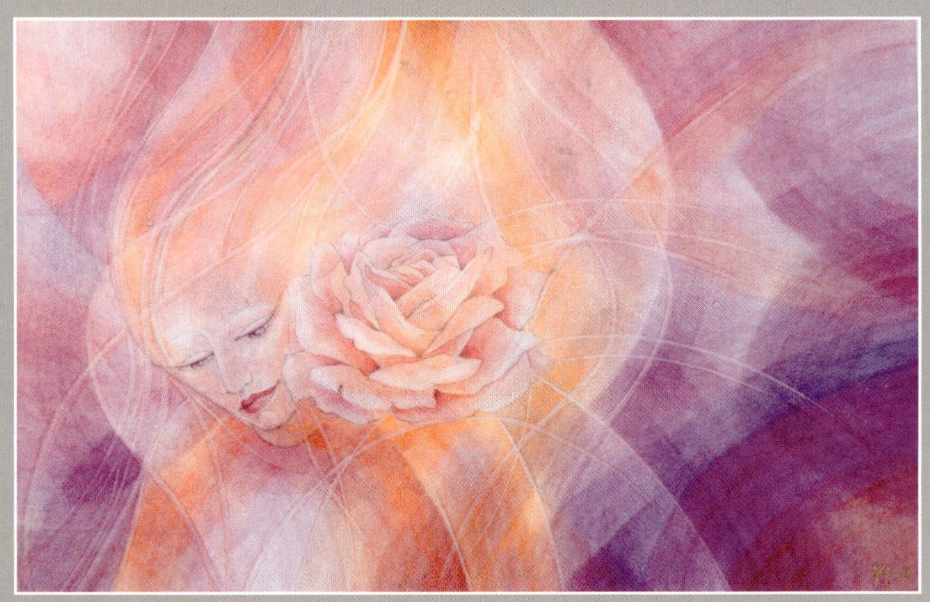

Rose Deva

Bridging the interface between worlds, she holds all – evoking unconditional love and wisdom, bringing harmony and peace into the soul of being....her perfume inviting the lover to return

The usual positive associations made about the colour red are that it is dynamic, powerful, tenacious, strong willed and pioneering. It is grounding, reviving, cheerful and passionate. Courage and liberation are qualities of red and it is also the colour of strength, rescue, survival, self -sacrifice and often associated with abundance and nobility. It is the colour of vitality and of blood; which is seen to carry life through the physical body. It is warming, generating and inviting. Red is a magnetic colour and draws towards itself.

Alternately it is a colour associated with anger, physical violence, destruction, lust, intolerance, shame and guilt. Red is about acting before thinking as well as irritation ie: inflammation that can manifest at both a physical and emotional level. There is an impatience to red and it can be pushy. It causes an instinctive and involuntary response and can be defensive and territorial. When red is not given permission to express itself, in a repression of anger or passion it can turn inward and become depression. Red, like fire burns fast and hot, destroying what lies in its path. Psychologically it can help to break through old and rigid belief systems making way for new ideas, much like the rain after a fire allows for strong growth of new plants.

Pink

I'm including pink as I feel it is an important aspect of the red ray. We may also refer to pink as the Ray of Love. When someone is in need of pink their issues are more than likely related to love in some aspect. Pink is to do with believing in love and accepting life's lessons as one's teachers. It is about surrendering to unconditional love allowing us to be receptive and responsive. Pink is a maternal colour and evokes a sense of nurturing and protection.

Love in its basic colour radiation is a rose pink of an indescribable hue and an unforgettable fragrance. It is the essence of all manifestation and is inbreathed with the solar breath whenever a man is receptive. Once his aura is prepared to receive and give it forth, the hues deepen and change with the manifestation of his aura. Love, therefore, may have many related shades from pale, pearly pink of an embryo down to deep rose red. The ray of love is the greatest because it has the essence of all things within it, and from it all things are made. Love is the whole of life.

A World within a World

It is also within the aspects of this colour that we can work with forgiveness. Unlike the strong passion of red, pink is softer, kinder, more sensitive, understanding and affectionate. Some of its other positive qualities are that it is faithful and often suggests fulfillment of one's potential. It is a supporting and nurturing colour and can be very beneficial in any situation where there has been assault, fear, betrayal and loss of trust and hope. Pink imbues us with a true love and compassion for humanity. This is also an aspect of the magnetic spectrum and like red draws towards itself.

Some of the negative aspects of pink include being too trusting, impetuous and immature. Sometimes it may appear as being over sensitive, over emotional and too cautious in matters of the heart. Pink may also act in the reverse and exhibit a slightly stiff and unusually strong and singular nature. It can sometimes show as a slightly unrealistic approach to life; hence the expression seeing life through roe coloured glasses and it continually searches for nurturing and support. Pink is even used in some prisons because it helps to reduce aggressive and violent behaviour. It has also been found to slightly effect energy by sapping the strength of inmates.

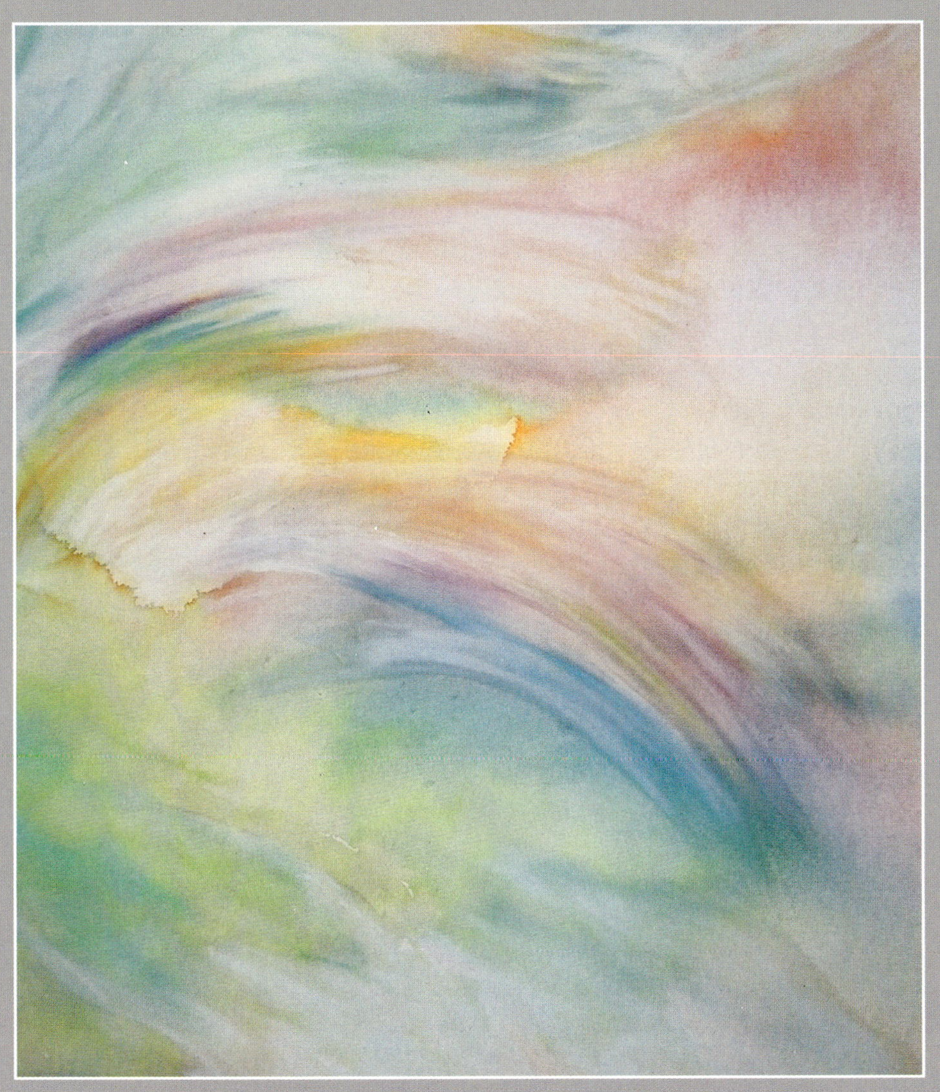

Etheric Waterfall

Orange

We associate this colour with the second or Naval Chakra. Whereas red is primarily about the energy for survival and the individual, orange relates to the energy of two and is about intimate or close relationships. It is focused more on our voluntary responses to others and very much about the expression of emotion. Here we have the combination of yellow and red and the inherent qualities within these colours plays a part in the way orange expresses itself.

The positive key associations with the colour orange include; joy; sociability; activity; strength; generosity; warm-heartedness; tolerance; fearlessness; justice; freedom; optimism; positivity; geniality; excitement and persistence. It is about using energy wisely. Orange also relates to our sexuality, inner freedom and the need for exploration. This colour is also seen as being an assimilator and within the physical body it acts to test what we have taken in and then either accepts or rejects it. It causes us to respond instinctively with wisdom.

The energy of orange can help with trauma and unblocking barriers. It encourages one to move through difficulty and feel a renewed sense of purpose and vigour. It does not work with the same aggressive energy as red and is more coaxing and gently stimulating. Orange is the colour of expansion and loves creativity. It is constructive, encouraging and illuminating. Orange in its gentler hues promotes activity quietly and allows for a greater caution before making a move or decision.

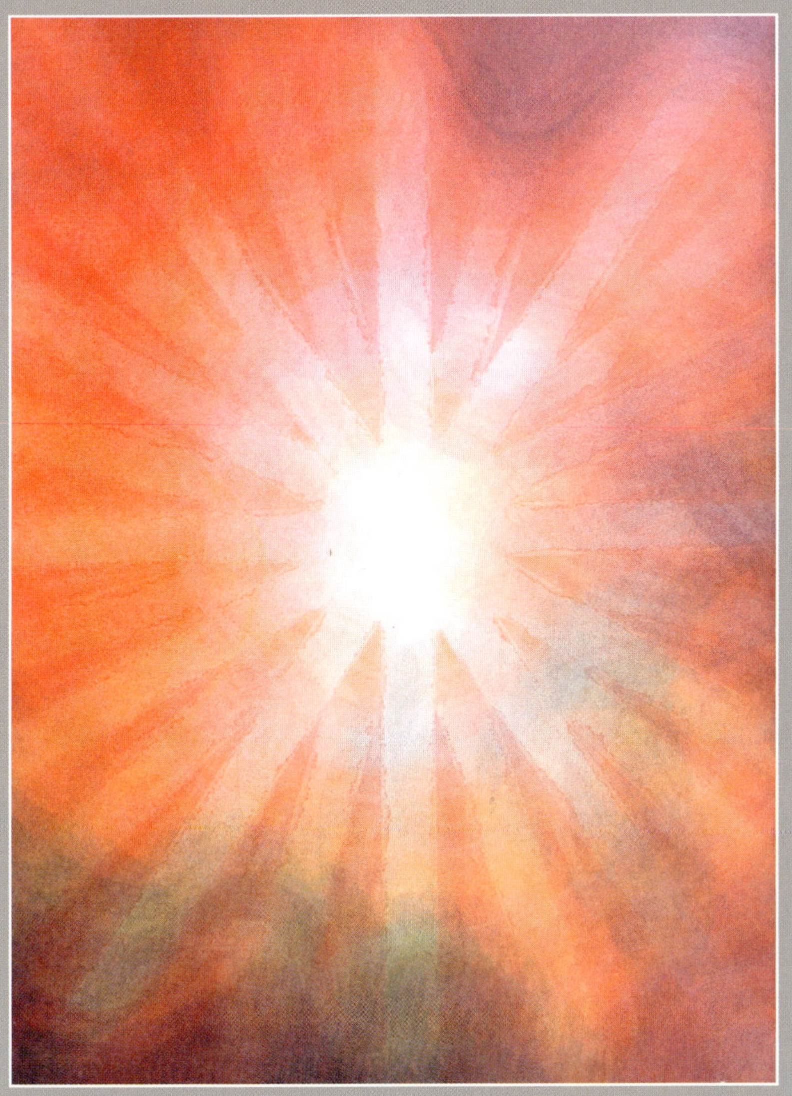

Morning Star

Inner light whose radiance illuminates darkness and brings guidance with insight

From a negative perspective, orange could have lost faith and does not believe in itself. It neither acts nor reacts and remains impassive.

It can sometimes also be restless; anxious; too ambitious and contradictory. Orange can view the world as unfair and find it very difficult to move forward. Often when one can't move forward, there is an inward hoarding of toxic emotions as well as an outward hoarding of material possessions. Orange can tend towards compulsive behaviour and never have a real sense of true potential. This could manifest as restlessness, lack of satisfaction and hyperactivity. When there is an imbalance, orange can come across as being too ambitious and takes on more than it can handle, eventually resulting in feelings of rejection. There could be an insidious sense of rivalry in much of its motivation.

In 'The Miracle of Colour Healing', Vicky Wall refers to her orange over orange bottle as the Humpty Dumpty bottle. She describes the etheric gapping that takes place in shock situations where the True Aura moves to the periphery of the body,

> The slip-road provided by the etheric [the ether around the body], where the divine spark may rest until help and healing have taken place. Through this etheric gapping there can be energy loss.

This experience is often accompanied by feelings of disorientation and the inability to 'Get oneself back together again'. By working with orange it can assist in the realigning of the body and aura and help one to heal the trauma and shock. Its gifts are wisdom and energy.

Yellow

Like red and orange, yellow belongs to the magnetic aspect of the spectrum and draws towards itself. It is associated with the Solar Plexus Chakra, which at both a physical and subtle level, deals with the way in which we digest life. Here there is a focus on the inter-relationship we have in a group context and our discernment when it comes to survival intuition. In other words it is the way we orientate ourselves in social circumstances.

It is at this level that we develop an acute awareness of other people's intentions, both positive and negative and we can then use our personal power to either deflect or absorb the energy. When yellow is working well we have a strong connection to our intellect and are able to use analytical and logical thought when making decisions or assessments. We can evaluate our alternatives and communicate in a productive way. Yellow is a creative colour and relates to the mind.

Some of yellow's positive attributes include; quickness and agility of mind; wisdom; expansion; tolerance; confidence; justice; honesty; joy; originality and rigor. This colour lifts one's spirits and holds the promise of new beginnings. It is symbolic of sunshine and life and is associated with new ideas. It not only thinks and decides quickly but also tends to act quickly. When yellow is fully aware of it's potential and power it has a high self esteem and sense of worth. Yellow is positive and works towards a goal with great optimism. By nature yellow is inquisitive and likes putting facts together. Much like the digestive system that this colour is also associated with, yellow loves connecting and networking.

It is a colour that is very comfortable in today's technological and media arenas. It is smart, perceptive, loves communicating and is a born investigator.

Some of yellow's negative qualities include being too analytical; critical; judgemental; confusing; talkative; ignorant and impatient. Yellow can be too inquisitive for its own good and the term 'curiosity killed the cat' would be very apt here. It can also be mentally manipulative and cleverly evade direct confrontation. Sometimes yellow will be the first to see and understand a situation but in many instances it lacks hindsight and does not employ its gift of perception well.

Yellow can appear hard hearted and uncaring at times because it insists on rational reason. At an extreme level, yellow can manifest as a fanatic who is quite prepared to achieve goals regardless of what others may want or think. At times yellow can result in mental and nervous exhaustion. Yellow enjoys a good argument but can also become argumentative, and lose focus. When yellow is off balance it can result in joylessness, lack of self-love, lack of self-worth, lording it over others, deceitfulness, insecurity, instability and discrimination.

Yellow in its splendour is happy, joyful and easy to be with. It is a font of wisdom and ideas and is always up to a mental challenge. It looks for the good in life and works to keep smiling even in difficult situations. Yellow looks for workable solutions to problems.

Green

The colour green falls in the middle of the rainbow spectrum and as such contains both the magnetic and electric aspects; yellow and blue. It is associated with the heart chakra and when in balance it reflects repose, healing and nature consciousness. Vicky Wall describes green as,

...nature's space giver in which the soul may stretch. It is the polarizer and centralizer of the being, bringing awareness of the true need and thereby giving the capability of decision with action.

Green gives the possibility of opening the heart to receiving and giving love. It is relaxing and invites a letting go and in the process peace and balance are experienced.

Some of green's positive attributes include; generosity; regeneration; hope; growth; discrimination; practicality; stability; progression; peace; loyalty; sensitivity; commitment; tactfulness and stability. Green forms a bridge between the warm magnetic colours of red, orange and yellow to the higher, electric energies of blue, indigo and violet. This colour is associated with the ability to make and conserve wealth. Green makes it possible to see both sides of any situation so it can be depended on for right judgement and compassion. Working with issues of love one can connect to all the other levels in order to grow spiritually and serve mankind in a positive way.

If we make an analogy between the green of a plant and ourselves, we see that it is the colour of growth and as a stem it holds the flower up to the light and the roots hold firm to the ground.

As we know green is the colour of chlorophyll and acts as a sunlight trap. It captures the sun's energy and stores it in the plant. Without green, the world we know would not exist. We obtain the energy we need for living from this solar energy, either by consuming the plants themselves or animals that eat the plants. Even the energy we obtain from fossil fuels like oil and coal is solar energy that has been trapped by plants millions of years ago. Chlorophyll acts to transform this light source into a utilizable form for all the inhabitants of our planet.

Paramhansa Yogananda writes in Autobiography of a Yogi -

Someday scientists will discover how man can live directly on solar energy.

Green is the colour that makes our world go round. It is no mystery then that this colour is associated with our heart chakra.

The negative aspects of green can be: too moralizing; too assertive; envious; over achieving; self-denying; self-suppressing; needing recognition; defensive; possessive; greedy; self-obsessed; unreliable; uncaring; deceitful; two-faced; irresponsible; immature.

When green is working well it realizes its true worth and the worth of others. It wishes to bring peace and balance to all situations. It perseveres and is committed to a world that exists with harmony and balance and is a place where everything is honoured and respected. Green trusts the process of life and generates new growth in all situations.

Blue

...We are now dwelling in thought upon the basic radiation, which itself is a quality of balance and coherence within the particles of vibratory life composing the earth and holding it in balance.

A World within Worlds

It is suggested that there is a particular quality of the colour blue that holds all creation. This colour is described as being like the blue of a clear night sky when there are a great multitude of stars. It feels alive, pure and tranquil. It reflects a great calm and reminds one of the steadfast and enduring quality of the creator. It is serene and radiates a peace that is beyond understanding.

Esoterically blue is associated with the throat chakra and it would be accurate to say that at a physical and auric level this colour is very significant for us. When in balance we feel at peace and inspired; we feel that we can trust life and we act with integrity and purpose. Blue is therefore a great healer and provides direction.

When we are unable to communicate our truth we are unable to bridge our connection at a soul level to the heavens, earth and animal kingdoms. Lack of communication and expression stifles creativity.

From a positive perspective blue is associated with; wisdom; spirituality; contemplation; loyalty; quietness; patience; truth; integrity; mental acumen; healing; purpose; calm; restfulness; discretion; confidence; intuition; idealism; bridging; communication; will power; sincerity; creativity; confidence.

Blue communicates its wisdom. It speaks from the head and the heart and often finds itself in the position of teacher. Blue can be trusted and does not rush into making decisions. It weighs things up carefully and considers the consequences of actions. The energy of blue is purposeful and brings peace and calm into difficult situations. Blue is associated with the Throat energy centre that expresses itself through vocal communication and creative expression of the self. This is a colour well suited to the media and broadcasting of any nature. It wishes to honour the higher will of the soul and through discernment is able to identify the difference between the individual will of the ego and G-d's will. Blue is caring and in as much as it communicates truth it is also very good at listening to others. This is a restful colour and makes space for contemplation and meditation in the midst of outer noise and disruption. Blue likes to be of service.

In its negative aspects blue can be introverted and disconnected. Some of the qualities it can manifest are an emotional instability; superstition; conceit; frigidity; lack of forgiveness; character weakness; sentimentality; remoteness; fear of direct confrontation; manipulation; spitefulness; moodiness; victim mentality; depressive tendencies; unexpressed emotions that turn in on themselves and become debilitating and depressive.

Blue is a transcendent colour bridging the seen and unseen worlds. It is connected to both clairvoyance and clairaudience and is a colour that helps to free us of material bondage so that we are able to connect more with our spiritual natures. This peaceful colour allows us to move more freely into the sacred space within.

Indigo

The colour indigo contains both blue and violet and as such also acts as a bridge. It is associated with the Third Eye Chakra and the Pituitary gland that enables the soul to perceive and recognize its chosen path and the way ahead. This part of ourselves enables us to gain access, knowledge and wisdom and to connect to our higher selves. It enables us to work with our clairvoyance and clairaudience (through the third eye Chakra) using our spiritual discernment.

This colour is in its positive aspects one of integration; redemption; practical idealism; clarity of perception; tolerance; fluency; co-ordination; sense of oneness; devotion; courage; obedience; reverence; structure.

When indigo is clear and working with purpose, it has the ability to create with foresight for the future because its gift is that of perception. It aspires to creating from its highest truth and works with the universal laws for the bettering of all life. Indigo is not easily dissuaded and will seek out the truth without withdrawing. It has spiritual strength and will uphold traditions and established belief systems.

The energy of indigo searches for that which is just and supports the rights of others. Indigo can be relied on in any emergency for a clear head and a strong sense of responsibility. This colour seeks the meaning of life and is open to exploration of new levels of experience, particularly the psychic dimensions. In many ways this is a very fluid colour that influences us to continually review our belief and thinking patterns and reminds us there is something more as well as another level of experience.

When indigo is not working in its truth and the energies are muddied and unclear, some of the qualities that may manifest are intolerance; lack of practicality; falsehoods and contradiction; lack of consideration; scattered thinking; idol worship and disintegration.

Indigo can become fanatical and try to impose its thoughts on others in a cruel and uncaring way. It chooses not to understand another's viewpoint and can be a bigot. When Indigo loses a sense of its direction, there is no hope and no structure or purpose. Directly related to this is the problem of addiction usually in the form of drugs or drink.

Indigo searches desperately to connect with spirit and purpose and by doing this it is attempting to find a quick access to greater perception. Unfortunately this is short- lived, harmful and the experiences cannot be grounded. Indigo can be self-sacrificing and totally devoted to teaching or order without regarding the bigger picture.

This is the darkest of the colour combinations being made of dark blue and dark violet. It invites one into the depths and also across the spiritual bridge.

Violet

This is the last of the visible spectrum colours and is associated with the crown chakra and pineal gland. Violet is made up of magenta and blue and therefore signifies the joining of heaven and earth. Purest white light enters through this crown portal and in turn constantly flows in a vertical fashion to all the other energy centres. It is the closest connection we have to the light of our spirit that is not divided. Violet is directly connected to the source and is committed to the service of true spirit. It reveres life and is spiritually dedicated. It is the 'I am that I am' colour and connects to the universal, spiritual network.

Violet is positively associated with mysticism; unification; enchantment; intricacy; transmutation; pure idealism; dedication; self-sacrifice; intuition; apperception; realization; true power; peace; visionary; indulgence; sensitivity; calm.

The energy of violet is such that it can sacrifice itself to benefit the greater whole. It carries the quality of leadership and self- mastery and prefers to always be the boss. It has the ability to be inspirational to others and original. Violet calms and brings peace to situations and has both poise and humility. This colour supports others by helping them to have a better sense of themselves. As a result their self-esteem and confidence improve.

In its negative aspects, violet can become; self opinionated; arrogant; snobbish; aloof; fanatical; treacherous; dominating; power hungry; perfectionist; ruthless; corrupt; belligerent; impractical; arrogant; dogmatic; depressive; evasive; immature; tyrannical.

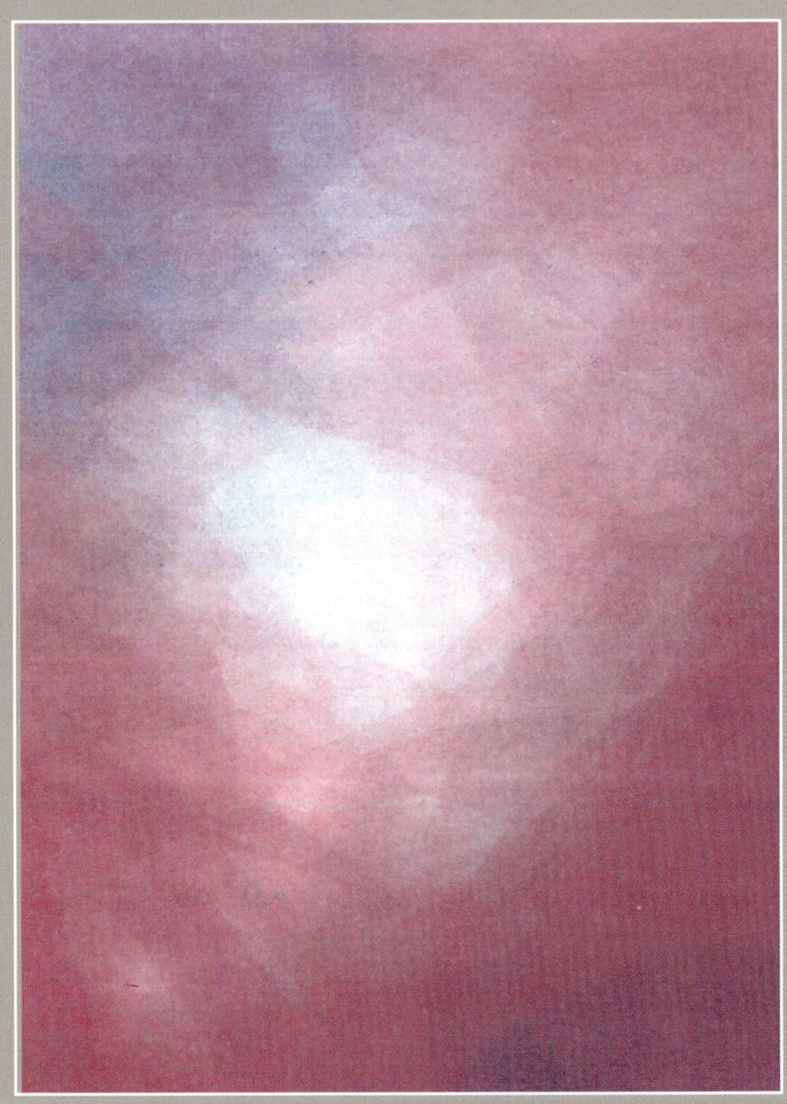

Crystal Cave

Reflecting back our own multifaceted natures – inviting us into her crystalline consciousness, we are offered the possibility of healing and raising ourselves to our fullest potential.

Violet is the great transformer and transmuter of the colour spectrum. It is linked with that which is magical and mystical and being a spiritual ray it offers protection on inner and outer journeying. It brings clarity and assists in helping us to make decisions and choices both peacefully and with purpose.

COLOUR AVENUES

The pure vibrational energies of light can be used therapeutically in a variety of ways. We need to remember that we are a manifestation of stepped down cosmic energy reflecting to a greater or lesser degree those higher energies that constitute our auric fields or subtle bodies. These colour rays of pure coloured light are celestial in origin and influence every aspect of who we are. When we specifically use colours for healing we are working to bring a molecular change within our bodies that will ultimately bring the harmony and balance back.

There are many ways to introduce colour; some of them require the assistance and guidance of a qualified therapist and others are based on common sense and good intuition. Some practitioners are able to tell just by looking at a client what colours are required to re-establish optimum health. They are naturally able to tune in at the auric level and see the disharmony or discolouring within the energy fields. This is certainly a gift that anyone can develop through compassion and a growing awareness of energy fields.

People's response to difficult or unpleasant situations is often to block their feelings and use alternate coping mechanisms, to the detriment of their well being. The result of this is that the energy flow to the relevant centre or chakra is distorted and slowed down and in some cases there is even a complete stop to the flow. This inevitably will affect the functioning of the centre and can lead to disease.

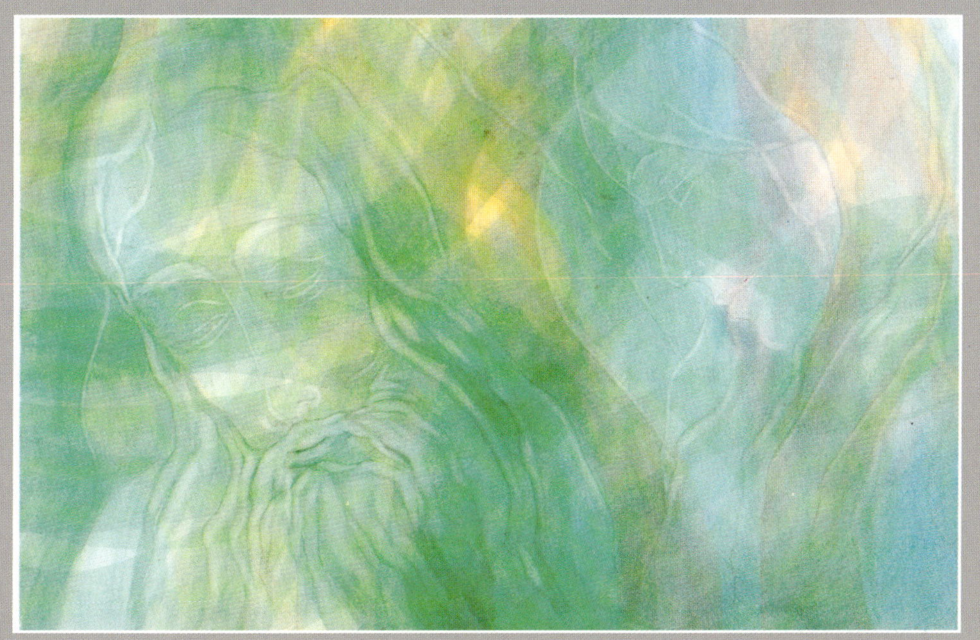

Journey of the Heart

An inner communication – a message of hope through change – a journey into new perspectives of love through forgiveness and the letting go of fear.

This process can be reversed using colour as the facilitator. One of the most powerful ways of doing this is to simply breathe colour. This is a type of meditation and is most beneficial when it is practiced early in the morning or just before going to bed. There are many techniques but the simplest is to just imagine breathing in different colours; imagining these in the form of light that infuses every cell of the body. It is good to work with this intuitively as well as focussing on each colour of the rainbow spectrum, directing the light to the corresponding energy centres ie; red to the base chakra, orange to the sacral etc. This can be very uplifting and acts as a colour tonic. It is also very powerful to use a mantra or affirmation attuned to each colour. The best way is not to try too hard but to simply follow the breath and allow oneself to be filled with soft coloured light.

During sessions I might suggest to clients that they imagine breathing in a soft, warm, coloured mist that spreads easily through their bodies. When they encounter any blockages or have a sense of stagnant energy they just let the light filter through, releasing the old energy as they breathe out. Our minds have such power that with breathing alone we can introduce those colours that will bring about effective and positive change.

Another way of introducing colour is by the process of thought transference. By focussing our attention on a specific colour we have the ability to transmit or channel that colour to another person - a little like absent healing which uses the universal energy field.

Visualization is also very much part of how the mind can be used to form or create images on one's inner screen or the mind's eye.

In this process the person who is doing the visualization is involved in actively creating an image that will be healing. Specific scenarios can be acted out in the imagination and symbolism can be imbued with colour and introduced to different parts of the body. It is a way in which we can give energy to something that has the possibility of becoming a reality. The clearer the image the greater the possibility that it can be actualised.

When we visualize certain colours we in turn produce those specific frequencies which when focussed on problem areas can result in psychological, emotional, spiritual and physical changes. Even when we just meditate on different sources of colour like paint pigments, crystals, flowers, food etc; this has the potential to enhance their inherent properties and effects. In addition to this, lasers, crystal wands, glass filters and kaleidoscopes all focus light which can direct the subtle energy of colour into the charkas.

Some practitioners use coloured lights that have been specifically modified. These are shone on different parts of the body with varying intensity depending on the problem that a client is experiencing. The degree of intensity and exposure time compensates for the deficiencies within the energy system.

As stated earlier it is always important to undergo these forms of colour therapy with a fully qualified practitioner.

Our best source of light is from the sun and in sensible doses this is the most natural way of receiving the full colour range of the spectrum. As we know it is not always possible to expose ourselves on a regular basis as many people live in parts of the world where daylight is shorter in the winter months.

Another factor is the difficulty some elderly and infirm people have to gaining access to the outdoors. In these instances light and colour can be introduced via special lamps or by focussing the available light onto different parts of the body using reflectors. These can be angled to refect the natural or filtered light.

Another wonderful way of introducing colour is in the form of coloured bags containing salt. These are exposed to sunlight or lamp light and can then be used by gently massaging the body with them. In a similar way water may be solarized in coloured glass. By exposing the water in the glass to sunlight it is imbued with the quality or frequency of the colour. With regard to thought transference this may be similarly used to potentize water with the thought of a specific colour. This is referred to as magnetizing the water.

There are different colour therapy systems using single and dual coloured bottles that aim to address the intrinsic way that colour works to vibrationally bring support and healing to the body, mind and spirit. The products are usually constituted of the purest, natural living energies of gems and plant essences. The intention behind these is deeply inspired and they have been created to meet the needs of our multi-dimentionality. This means that the focus for bringing these colours through in this way is so that we can work directly on the currents of energy that converge within us through our subtle body systems in order to create balance and harmony. Consultations using these colour modalities involves taking one on a very special journey of exploration and discovery into the real self with its unique gifts, challenges and present purpose.

These beautiful bottles combining the finest of oils sitting in equal part on the surface of the purest water are designed to work directly on the body with its electro-magnetic field and are generally applied to the skin over the areas that the colours relate to. Because the skin is semi-permeable it allows the therapeutic colours, herbs, essences and extracts contained in the bottles to enter the blood stream, through to the lymph and immune systems, thus affecting the entire healing response of the body.

There are also colour tincture bottles that work with the body and hold the healing vibration of the colours. These are taken orally as a liquid by placing a few drops into a small glass of water and can also be applied to the skin in the form of a cream.

Beyond and working with the physical body are the higher energy systems that are composed of matter with a different frequency, even though they exist in the same space. It is within the first couple of these subtle fields that different colour products have been created to work specifically. They protect the life energy, heal and clear as well as have the capacity to act as a catalyst for freeing inner vision or insight. They are used by placing a few drops in the palm of the left hand, rubbing the hands together and then passing the hands through the aura.

In this range are a set of bottles that help us re-connect with those higher aspects of ourselves that need to emerge. They enable us to go more deeply in our meditation and assist in the giving and receiving of healing. As well as this they help to take us to a place of stillness and peace where we can connect with our Source, aiding Karmic Absolution and the release of universal love.

They too are applied by putting a few drops onto the left wrist pulse and the vapours are then passed around the head and through the auric sphere.

Another series of colour therapeutics have been designed to specifically mirror the soul of Africa. They include warm earthy colours and mostly shades of the same colour ie; dark gold over pale gold, gold over copper, pale pink over copper etc. The rest include African greens - vibrant olives and dark forest greens; African sunset and deserts colours; toffee reds and shades of gold; deep rose pink and lavender, royal blue and rich coral. There are some that are dual colours like copper over deep turquoise which helps to feed information from the depths of Atlantis into the Earth's consciousness. Southern hemisphere essential oils, gems and plant extracts have been used and there are two sets of chakra bottles - the traditional colours plus a new set as well as essences that can be used as room clearers - sprayed in the hand and inhaled or gently taken over the head so that the energy permeates the Auric field.

African Angels is the name given to colour therapy bottles that also contain African aromatherapy oils, plant extracts and gemstones. Interestingly enough as they were being birthed a little book entitled About Angels and G-d was being launched in South Africa and it was discovered a short while later that the messages that had come through in relation to the twelve bottles was perfectly aligned to the essences and colour of the African angel paintings in the book. So it was that a powerful link through the medium of colour was made.

For information on different products refer to the Colour Therapy websites at the end of the book

A colourfully balanced eating regime should include on a daily basis each colour of the spectrum. Red foods are energizing, grounding, helpful for recharging our magnetic energies and strengthening our immune systems. They can also be good for the blood. Foods that reflect this ray include red pepper; chilli; raddish; red apples; all red fleshed and skinned berries; beetroot; red cabbage; red plums; tomatoes etc.

Orange foods are particularly helpful for building up the immune system and like red foods these are energizing and grounding. Both red and orange are also good for detoxifying and cleansing. Foods that reflect this ray include oranges; orange skinned grapefruit; cling peaches; golden plums; royal jelly; mangoes; paw paw; butternut; pumpkin; orange peppers; carrots; gooseberries etc.

Yellow foods are especially beneficial for detoxifying and for maintaining a good digestive system. The colour yellow is an uplifting one and is associated with the solar plexus chakra which governs the stomach and upper digestive tract including the liver and gall bladder. The foods that are this colour can be slightly acidic and include lemons; grapefruit; melons; pineapple; yellow plums; gooseberries; bananas;yams; golden corn or sweet corn; yellow peppers; squash; egg yolks; butter etc.

Green foods are important in terms of balancing, draining, strengthening and cleansing, particularly the blood. The colour green is associated with the heart chakra so these foods would support the healthy functioning of the heart system. In nature green is always associated with new beginnings and it is chlorophyll that traps the vital energy of the sun and converts it to food.

It is important to ensure that green foods are a large part of our daily intake and these would include all dark, leafy, green vegetables; cucumbers; green skinned courgettes; green peppers; watercress; green skinned apples; avocado pears etc.

Blue foods are a little more rare but it is nevertheless important to include an aspect of this colour for the overall well being of the body. Blue is regarded as a calming and cooling colour and some foods which are associated with this ray are the blue skinned berries like blackberries; bilberries; blueberries; black skinned grapes; plums; damsons and some asparagus etc.

The indigo foods are closely linked to the blue foods and can be helpful when needing to energise and focus on brain function and nervous system, in other words those areas governed by the brow chakra.

Finally violet foods again are very similar to the blue and indigo rays and would also include all the dark berries like grapes and blackberries as well as dark purple broccoli, red cabbage, aubergines and beetroot. All of these are rich in elements including magnesium which are essential to all brain and mental functioning.

There are obviously situations where there may need to be professional guidance and one should always eat sensibly and with awareness of the particular needs of the whole of one's being.

These colour rays of pure coloured light are celestial
in origin and influence every aspect of who we are

WORLDS WITHIN WORLDS

Working creatively with colour and imagery through guided meditation and visualization.

As soon as I reached G-d 's unity, I became a bird whose body was of Oneness and whose wings were of Everlastingness. I went on flying until I reached the expanse of eternity and gazed upon the Tree of Oneness

Abu Yazid Bastami - 9th Century Sufi Poet

We've all got what it takes to make a positive difference, it is just that so many of us have forgotten how powerful we really are.

Over the past eleven years, I've found that incorporating colour therapeutically, other than painting, is to 'think and breathe it'. Taking someone on a guided visualization using colour can evoke deep-seated emotional responses and memories. It allows for a free, associative connection between specific colours and what they represent. The combination of music and imagery is very powerful and it works at an energetic level to source and release difficulties and trauma.

Often I use meditation as a doorway to visualization. It acts to still the mind and settle the body, making possible a clearer intent. Through it one can be guided to entering an inner space of tranquility and greater connectedness to the 'source' of one's being. It is from this 'still centre', that we can safely and gently be taken on an inner journey.

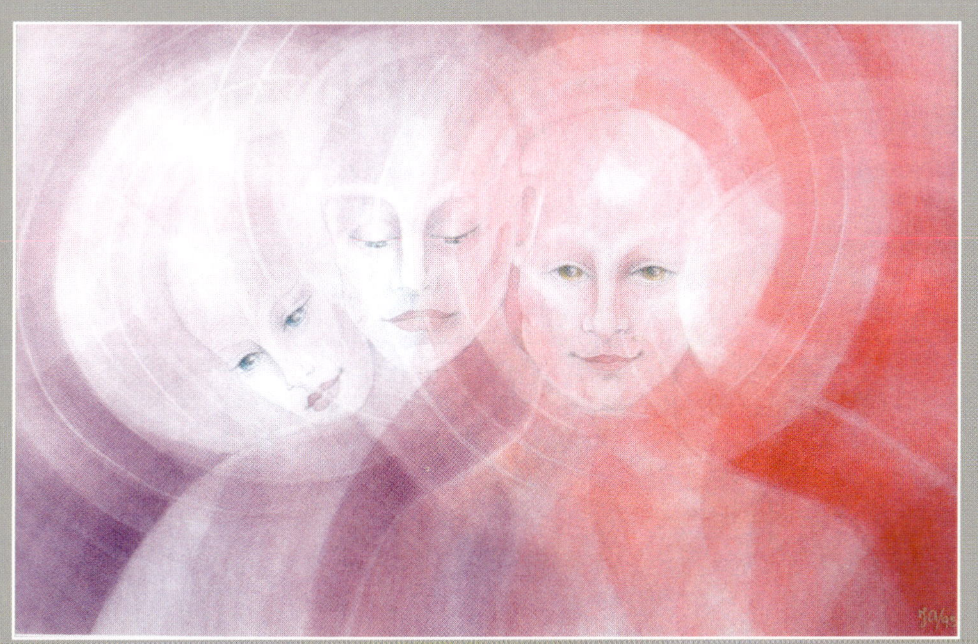

Watchful Friends

A gathering of healing souls united in the purpose of repairing the integrity of the physical and subtle bodies.

If we look at the nature of energy, this state has a higher vibrational quality or resonance to the ordinary, everyday state of our continuous 'inner chatter'. The Law of the Universe is such, that matter of a lower vibrational nature, can only be raised by matter of a higher vibrational nature.

In other words, when in a meditative state, the space we've entered becomes 'safe' and 'sacred'. If, through the visualization, we find ourselves remembering something difficult, this 'safe' space, allows us a certain objectivity to identify and experience the cause of imbalances. It allows for greater wisdom to shine on the situation and focus on difficulties. The result is greater compassion and understanding of the patterns that play through our lives and holds the possibility of experiencing deep inner peace.

Guided visualization and meditation help to open up our intuitive natures, and gain insight during our daily living. This allows our spirits to fantasize and explore constructively. Working in this way illumines the shadow side of our psyche and we have the possibility of recognizing and connecting with the hitherto 'unknown' agendas and motivations behind our repetitive negative patterns. Here we can give credence and respect to our creative minds and in doing so become more balanced as we attempt to live in this left-brain orientated society.

If we consider again, that everything in the known and unknown worlds is made up of energy, and that all energy acts in relationship, then everything is an expression of that energy and exists at a specific vibrational level. The energy of thought may be enhanced or lowered, simply through intention. In other words, a 'thought' is a creative impulse and we can change the 'pattern' or 'relationship' of the energy flow within us by changing what we think and ultimately believe.

Going back to the image of the 'broken mirror' of the Divine, we can choose to reflect the light or not. In essence we can consciously choose to work with those thoughts and images that will grow us, ennoble us and keep us true to ourselves. This does not imply that in life we will not feel, or be faced with pain or difficulty, but if we hold true to ourselves, we can meet it authentically and not through responses that are governed by entrenched belief systems and negative patterning.

Through visualization and imagery, we have a tool for enhancing the quality of our lives, and the possibility of healing at the deepest level. More than this, we gain insight through our dreaming and fantasy into 'the worlds within worlds'. It offers a safe place for releasing, resting, recharging and re-gathering our energies. It is a process of re-empowerment.

Just as there are specific techniques that support the best use of different mediums and activities, there are also formulations for achieving and experiencing the best results in guided journeying or visualization. Primarily, all that is required is the inner permission to take yourself on an adventure where you may meet all the different aspects playing through your life. These may include the child, teacher, wise person, victim, abuser, magician, mystic etc. It is only when we have gathered the rich reward of our wisdom that we come to know ourselves, embracing all that we are. Then we can begin to manifest through clarity and intention our special blend of magic along the paths of life.

When beginning a meditation or visualization, it's always important where possible, to sit with one's spine erect but not tense. If you are in a chair always allow your hands to rest comfortably and make sure that you have both feet on the floor.

Having an inner attitude of attention and softness helps to maintain wakefulness but in a relaxed manner. Try to ensure that you will not be disturbed through the course of the guidance. Making your outer space sacred is also helpful, this can be achieved by lighting a candle and saying a blessing.

It can be very helpful to invite a friend to talk you through the process, but this is not absolutely necessary. If you do choose to work with someone, make sure that they have a peaceful presence and a voice you enjoy listening to. This person would obviously need to be very aware and sensitive to you and to what is required, as they may need to pause or vary the tone of their voice slightly from time to time.

An alternative is that you pre-record the journey for yourself, which gives you the freedom to relax more fully as well as being able to do the particular meditation whenever the need arises.

I have used the following meditations in groups and for individual session work over the past ten years. They all include a journey, imagery, colour and meeting different levels in oneself. But the most important thing to remember is that the journey is always unique to each person and it's the individual's particular experience of the words that create the unfolding and reality of each story. This then is what is going to allow the different emotions to surface. In many ways this must always be seen as a continuing process and each step toward healing into wholeness is as important as the next.

Meditation

Merging with your Radiant Self

Make sure you are sitting comfortably and will not be disturbed. Gently close your eyes and allow your whole being, body, thoughts and feelings to just soften and relax. Feel yourself letting go into this moment and as you do so, begin to just observe your breathing. Don't try to change it in any way, just allow it.

Now with each out breath, focus on letting go of all that has gone before this moment and with each in-breath be aware of the new possibilities that are held within each moment. Remember, everything in nature dies on the out-breath and all that is born is born on an in-breath.

Continue to surrender to the feeling of peace and relaxation - letting go of any extraneous thoughts and associations. There is no need to attach to any of them, because they are not who you are.

Within this silence, begin to imagine yourself completely enveloped in the finest, golden, gossamer net. It has a beautiful radiance to it and you feel completely protected. Here you may ask that whatever negative energy is held within your energy-field, be spun out and that only 'light' and 'love' filter through this fine net.

As you breathe in, breathe in truth of the highest order and as you breathe out breathe out all that is not of this truth. Continue doing this until you feel completely at peace and held within an inner quiet.

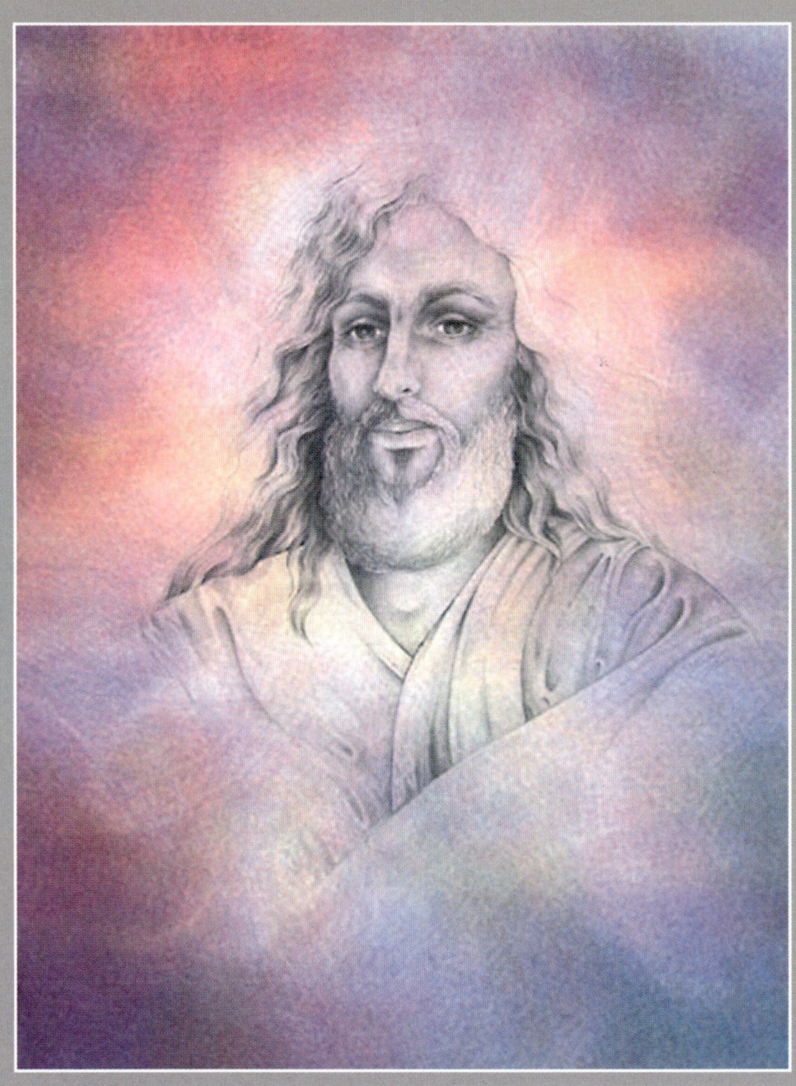

Djwal Khul
Supporting and encouraging with love as we learn to merge our auras with the aura of G-d. 'The Heart within the Heart'.

We are now going to go on a journey to meet with your Radiant Being or Higher Self. This being knows everything about you and has a great and unconditional love for you. Their soul purpose is to assist and support you as you embrace your life's purpose. This is your special journey so allow yourself to be open and guided by your 'truth'.

Gently become aware of yourself standing on the bank of a large, slow-flowing river at dawn. The world is just beginning to awaken to the first birdsong, and the air is fresh and clean. There's a faint mist sitting on the water and everything feels pregnant with new possibility.

Your senses are keenly alive and you feel the universe breathing life into everything around you. You too, feel yourself being breathed by the universe and as you look across the water, there is a murmuring of sacred breath rippling gently upon the surface, then all is still–perfectly still.

This stillness is within you and you merge with it and are not separate from it.

Within this stillness, you feel timeless and spaceless. You lift your face to the sun, which, in all its golden splendour has risen above the water and has become a brilliant orb of golden light. You find you can look directly into it and before long you begin to discern a great being emerging from it.

As your eyes become accustomed to the luminosity of this being, you begin to notice that rays of the most spectacular colours are streaming from their body of light. They are now standing just before you, pulsating with colour and radiating so much love and beneficence that you feel totally blessed with the grace of 'All That Is'.

There is so much light around you that you are no longer able to discern where you begin or end. You are only aware in this moment that you are both joined at the heart centre and your bodies are merging into One Great Radiance of light and colour.

There is no division or separation and you have become your 'radiant self'. Your consciousness is expanding with each breath and you experience being eternal. It feels as if you have entered a vast velvety silence of the purest peace and total surrender.

Allow yourself to be acutely aware of any energy shifts that may be taking place. Simply observe them with no wish to attach to an outcome.

Remind yourself that the way to return to this connection is always through the well of silence and stillness. This is the way that you can avail yourself of your inner guidance at any moment through the day.

For a moment you reflect with deep gratitude for this meeting and whilst still holding the radiance of the light within your heart, you gently begin to bring your attention and awareness fully back to the room you're sitting in. Take as long as you need and let your breath bring you into the space.

Only when you are ready, gently open your eyes and remain still for a while before moving into the rest of your day.

Remember that being mindful as you go about your daily work helps to reconnect you with the source of your own light and peace.

Allow yourself to be open and guided by your 'truth'

Meditation

Sacred Throne

Prepare yourself by ensuring you will not be disturbed and then settle yourself in an upright sitting position. Make sure that your back is straight and your body relaxed. Always keep your legs and your arms uncrossed, particularly if you are seated on a chair, as this ensures that your feet are both flat on the floor and your hands open to receiving.

Begin by simply following your breath and allowing a deep sense of calm to enter. With each in-breath you breathe in life, possibility and healing and with each out-breath you let go of anything that may be burdening you. Continue to just observe and repeat those thoughts till there is an inner-quiet and you feel centred.

Within the stillness you begin to focus your attention inwardly on a simple candle flame. This is quite still and as you look at it you notice how it contains every colour of the rainbow. Slowly you begin to feel yourself being drawn into its very centre. This happens very naturally and you have no fear. On the contrary, you willingly allow yourself to merge completely with the flame and release all negativity and expectation. You are freed of any mis-information you may have of yourself and the world. You experience a deep sense of relief and lightness and your conscious connection to this reality, for this time, simply disappears. You are now surrounded by violet flames and begin to feel lighter, completely cleansed through and transformed.

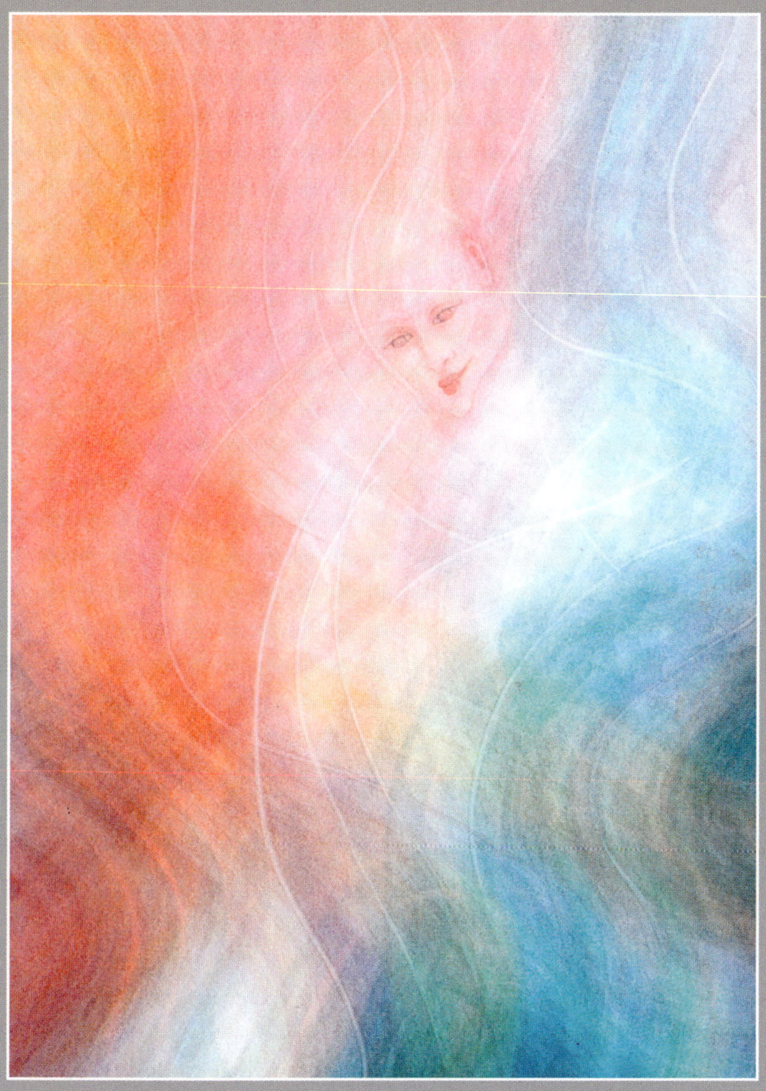

Nature Deva – Gabriella

The sound of golden coloured water gurgling over rounded rocks. Birds, butterflies and dancing light - the air clean and rich with the scents of greenery. She was there in the energy of love. Gabriella was the name of this committed caretaker.

When it feels right, step out of the flames. Your consciousness is greatly expanded and as you look at your beautiful body of light, you find that you are adorned in celestial robes. These are made of very beautiful and flowing colours and they spread all around you. Look closely at the particular colours and just get a sense of their quality and purpose. What do they symbolize for you?

Now you begin to move your attention to the surroundings. Look around you and find that you are standing on the shore of a very beautiful, small island, which appears to be suspended in a glistening sea. Above, the sky is like a crystal-clear sapphire blue dome. Just stand for a moment, drinking in the tranquility.

Before long you begin to hear music. You feel the sun directly overhead and there is the gentlest of breezes. You are drawn to an area in the centre of the island. Here you find a small clearing surrounded by trees and flowers. In the clearing is a natural rocky platform, with a large velvet cushion. This cushion has exactly the same colours as your robes and you begin to understand that this is your special place. You move towards the rocks and sit down.

As you sit down, you feel as though you are the centre of the island. Everything surrounding you is honouring and supporting your being and you're filled with a deep sense of gratitude and anticipation.

Sit quietly for a while, connecting with the immense feeling of peace. Here is the access to greater wisdom and you are invited to ask any questions relevant to your current life.

As you ask questions, the answers just seem to bubble up. Each answer will bring with it a symbolic gift that you may place somewhere in your body for safekeeping. These gifts may be anything that appear to you and it's not necessary that you understand what they represent right now. Just be open to receiving.

The wisdom of your Greater Self is available to you and you can make an affirmation or wish at this time. As you allow the wish to arise, you repeat it three times.

Gradually you allow the scenery to gently disappear. Picture yourself in your flaming celestial robes slowly taking on a more solid, physical form. Nothing of the experience is lost or diminished and you feel very much at peace and in harmony. You clearly remember the messages that you've received, as well as the gifts from spirit. You know that whenever there is a difficulty in your life, you can call on this wisdom and allow the gifts of symbolism to guide and support you.

Very gently, and in your own time, bring your awareness fully back into the room in which you are sitting. With a joyful heart you sense your wonderful body and the life that's coursing through your veins. Flex your fingers and toes and open your eyes as if you are seeing for the very first time.

Ascending Meditation

Having settled yourself comfortably either in a chair or on the floor, ensure that your spine is erect and your head held upright. Allow your whole body to relax, and feel yourself letting go of all tensions that may be remaining. As you breathe in, you breathe the thought of softness and as you breathe out, let go of any difficulties or negative associations.

Just follow your breath till you feel you are no longer controlling it and you will gradually begin to experience being breathed by the universe.

As you relax more and more, you begin to have the understanding that everything that has happened in your life so far, has been teaching you to love unconditionally. You see that all your experiences, though at times painful and hard, have brought you to this now-point. In this moment you sense that you are being held and loved and there is neither criticism nor judgement. Here you feel ready and poised to take the next step forward, whatever that may involve, knowing that it holds the possibility of you moving forward with an expanding heart.

All those that have been there for you and those who still wait to support you, are encouraging you to turn to them and ask about life. If there are any particular suggestions that you have at this time, ask within and allow the answers to come through. Know that while you remain in the light, those answers will always be for your highest purpose.

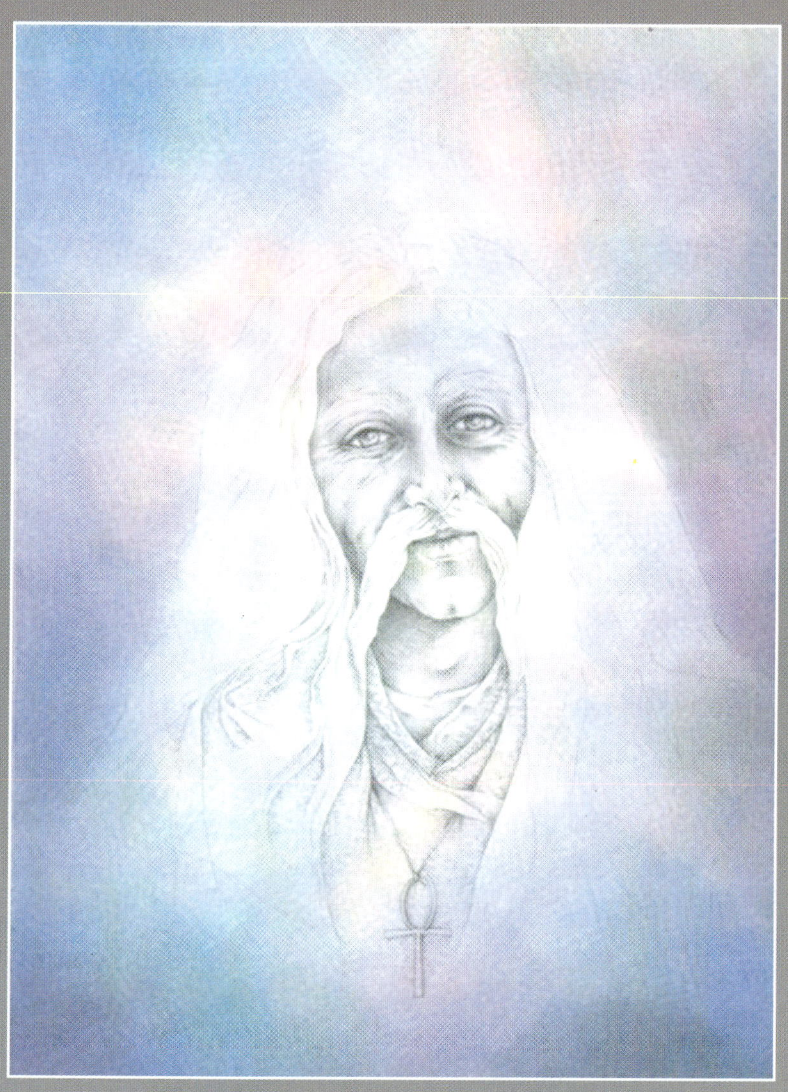

Serapis Bey

Wisdom glowing like lamplight in the dark beckoning and guiding those who have wandered away from the heart, back home to the Beloved.

You are now invited to ascend a very special mountain. As you look ahead, you see a long and winding path that snakes up the mountain, past boulders and many different types of terrain. You experience a little apprehension, but feel committed to making this journey.

Initially you find the ascent tiring, but this is soon replaced by a feeling of excitement and you begin to meet this challenge with joy. You enjoy the feeling of your body working and there is a deep gratitude within for this wonderful vehicle.

As you climb higher, the air feels cleaner and you begin to feel a lot lighter. You notice everything around you; the rocks, plants, bird and animal life, but most importantly, you notice how much a part of all this you feel. There's a different kind of sense filling you now and it seems to be growing from your solar plexus region. You are beginning to feel strong in yourself and powerful, simply because you exist and belong in this place.

Gradually you come to a point where you can see that you're not very far from the top of the mountain. With great determination, you inhale deeply and within a short time you find yourself at what feels like the top of the world. As you look around, you see everything at your feet, so to speak, covered by a faint mist that gives it an almost other-worldly reality.

For this moment, this is your mountain and you choose to explore further. As you look ahead you become aware of a very beautiful temple. This is your sacred temple, so you can allow it to become whatever you imagine. One of the distinctly noticeable things about it is that it is surrounded by clouds of continually changing colours and that each of these colours has a particular sound. These sounds together form the most exquisite, ethereal music you have ever heard. For a while this almost takes your breath away as you realize this is your music and these are the colours of your celestial robes.

As you drink this all in, you notice a golden light emanating from the centre of the temple. You walk towards it and climb several steps that lead you through an archway. The music is like soul food and as you move to the centre of the building everything about your life becomes clear. You remember your purpose and have a great sense of gratitude for the lessons you've learned. Your whole being is infused with light and music and at the deepest part of who you are you know you are a part of G-d, a part of the abundance of All That Is and at the level of soul your needs are always met.

Inwardly give thanks for that which you have received here, and now leave the Temple and find a place on the mountain where you can sit quietly before returning.

Meditation
losing yourself to love

Settle yourself comfortably in a sitting position either on the floor or in a chair. Ensure that your spine is straight and that your head is not falling either backward, forward or to either side. It helps to imagine that a fine, invisible thread is pulling it gently upward from the crown.

Allow your arms to rest against your body and your hands to be relaxed. It does not matter whether they are palm up or down. If you are seated, have your feet flat on the floor.

As you close your eyes, scan your entire body for areas of tension and allow a feeling of softness to take its place. Focus especially around the eyes, mouth and jaw area. Just allow the muscles to relax even if you need to slightly drop the jaw and open the mouth.

Begin observing and following your breath, gradually allowing yourself to be breathed naturally. Don't try to change it in any way. Simply observe.

You will begin to have the sense that the universe is now breathing with and through you.

Gently move your focus of attention to just above your navel. As you do so, a soft golden radiance emanates from this area, and like the finest mist it spreads itself in a cocoon shape around and just beyond your body. This brings with it a deep feeling of calm and peace at the same time as anchoring and protecting you as you begin to journey inward.

Imagine yourself walking on soft, warm sand. You feel received by it and

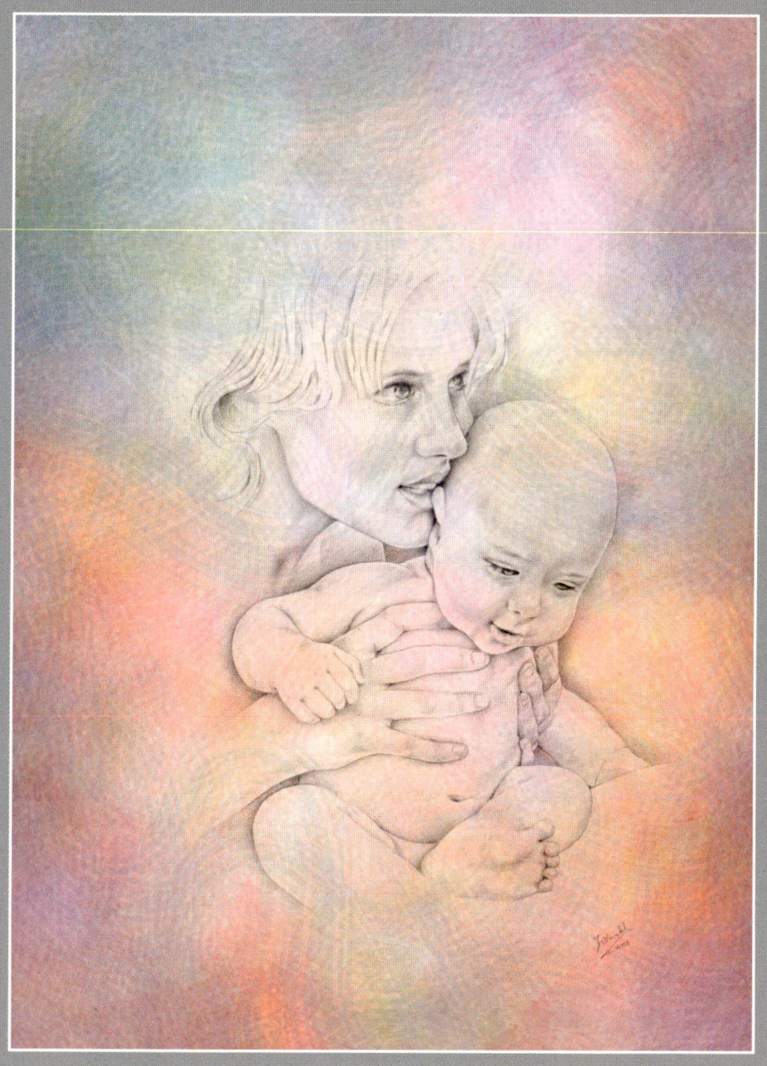

Modern Madonna

The Goddess expressing herself eternally through the loving embrace of all mothers.

as you take each new step, you're aware that dry sand is already beginning to fill the footprint you left before.

Your body is naked and you can feel the sun's rays on your skin. As you look around, you realize that you are on a secluded part of a beach. The sound of the waves crashing onto the rocks nearby plus the odd cry of a seagull, fills your ears and you feel absolutely free and at peace. Your heart expands with each sigh of the ocean. You experience immense gratitude and feel blessed by the grace of 'All that Is'.

As you look to the right, you notice that there is a protected little cove with its own rock pools. You wander over and sit in a shady spot, resting against a large, upright rock. From this vantage point you have a view of the entire beach and see that it is completely private.

As you lean back against the solid support of the rock, you can hear the water playing and gurgling amongst the pebbles in the rock pools. In a blissful reverie, you close your eyes and drift off. You are aware of looking at yourself resting against the rock. The difference is that your consciousness seems clearer, brighter and more colourful. You are light, and as you look directly into the heart of the sun, you find that you begin to glow more brightly.

You know your body is safe as it rests in the cove and you decide to glide up beyond the beach and over the ocean. You feel limitless and as you look down at the area you have just risen above you begin to see much more. There are beautiful mountains, rivers running into the sea, land with buildings, animals, people and vegetation.

You understand that as small as everything appears, you, too, are part of that, but you are also free to experience this expanded and higher view. As you survey the scene below, you're filled with an immeasurable love and respect for all life. You see how everything is inter-linked and inter-connected.

With this, you continue to expand as you move higher and without losing your focus on the planet, you begin to sense and recognize that you are just one of a myriad of other light beings around you.

Here there are no boundaries and you and the other celestial beings around you, merge, sharing the same level of consciousness.

You are one with all that emanates from the source and you have a particular focus at this moment. Your sole desire and focus is to assist the Earth as she moves into a higher level of her own consciousness.

With one intention, you and the collective soul of which you are a part, lovingly manifest the most delicate and subtle violet light and direct this at the Earth, totally enveloping her and all that are part of her. Your intention is that this violet light works to transform and transmute negative energy within all the energy fields of all beings, permeating through to every living cell.

As you observe this beautiful little planet, you see that all of life is being suffused by this light and the result is a gradual re-awakening and remembering of each one's soul purpose. As this happens, you notice that shadows are lightly moving out of the auras of every living being, including the body of the Earth. These shadows all merge into one and as they move towards the light, they simply change as they become part of the light.

It feels as though the Earth is sighing and letting go of that which has burdened her and no longer serves her. As you observe this, you and your Soul body, manifest a soft green ray of light and direct this around the Earth.

You sense that as it touches the heart of all, it evokes and encourages the qualities of balance, harmony, co-operation and healing. Something miraculous now takes place, as the most beautiful soft, pink light of unconditional love, now glows from the centre of the Earth. Everything begins to radiate this and it feels as if all life has been washed through.

At this point you decide to re-enter the Earth's vibrational field and with the greatest love and respect, you pinpoint your focus on your physical body as it rests against the rock by the sea. You do not feel that you are separating from your celestial family, but rather that you are returning for the specific purpose of lovingly supporting the positive transitions of the Earth through your thoughts and deeds.

As you return, your essential body of light gently rests back into your physical form. Your journey is almost complete. Slowly become aware of your body and its sensations. Listen to the sounds around you and allow them to bring you fully back into the room.

Sense your body in the chair, or on the floor and begin to focus your attention once more on following your breath. Very gently and in your own time, flex your toes and fingers and gently open your eyes. Practice seeing the world around you with softened vision.

Meditation

Walking into the Rainbow

Prepare yourself for going inward. Make sure you are sitting with your spine erect, whether you are sitting on a chair or on the floor. Imagine that your head is being slightly lifted from the centre at the top by an invisible thread. You are relaxed, but not too relaxed and gently closing your eyes bring your attention to focus on your breathing.

As you observe your breath, don't change it in any way, but simply follow it through your nostrils to your lungs and then out again. After a while you will have the sensation that you are being breathed.

With each in-breath, breathe in the idea of birth, newness and healing and with each out-breath just feel yourself releasing tension, anxiety and all that is no longer of benefit to your well being. In your mind allow it to become a prayer of surrendering.

When you feel you have centred and cleared, remind yourself that the journey you are about to go on is yours and that whatever comes up for you is valid and meaningful, even if at a rational level it may not make sense right now. You feel at ease and at peace.

No sound or thought is distracting you and your inner calm is reflected by the outside world.

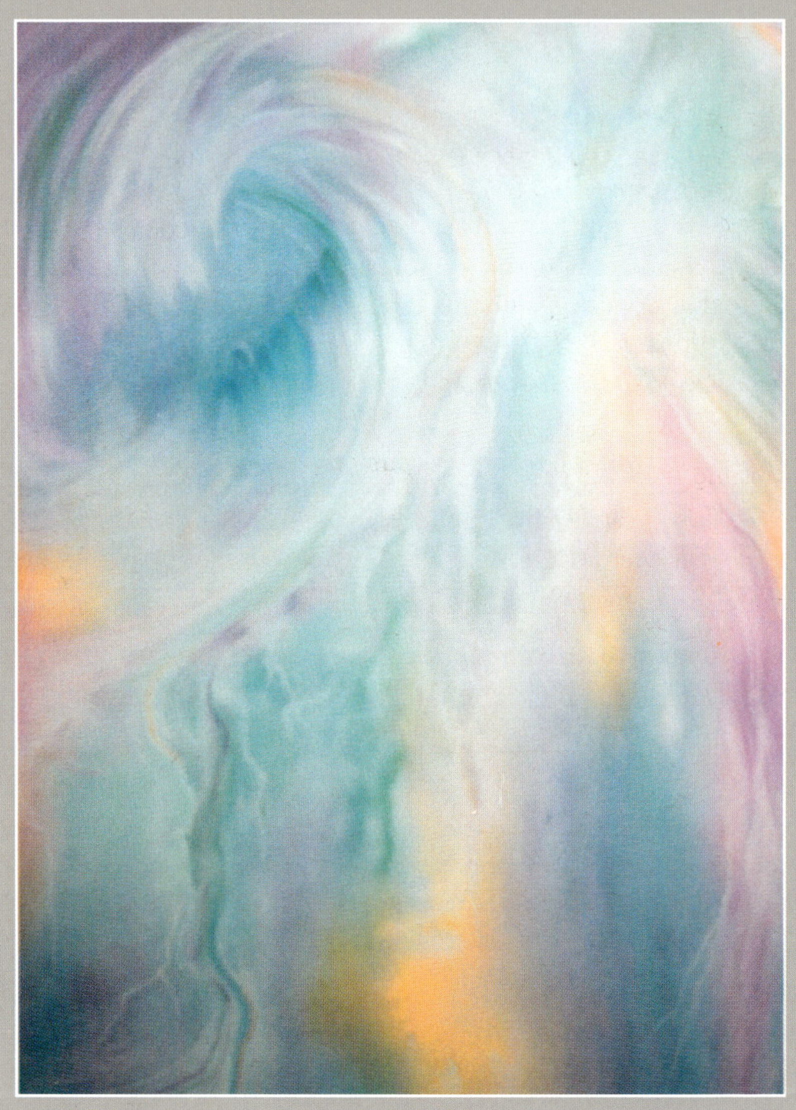

Air

In spaceless - space and timeless - time, these are the colours of our story.

You find yourself walking barefoot on a path where the stones are all covered by a soft, cool layer of green moss and lichen. There are trees on either side and leaves carpet the forest floor, as dappled sunlight plays through the trees. Every now and then you become aware of the movement of little creatures. You feel light and free and very much part of the forest. It's not difficult to understand the different bird songs, or the sounds of all that inhabit this place. The myriad shades of green and brown help you feel grounded and relaxed.

You walk towards the sound of running water and before long you come to a clearing where there is a small foot- bridge over a stream. As you look around, you notice that the weather seems different over the bridge on the other side, where there is a fine, blue mist. From where you are standing it is not clear as to what you may find.

You decide to continue and are free from any anxiety or fear. Something in you reminds you that all is well and that you can explore further quite safely. You feel both excited and curious.

As you step onto the bridge and walk into the mist, the sun breaks through and initially everything around you has the most incredible golden glow. At the point when you reach the other side, the whole world looks different. An enormous rainbow of light has been laid down over the land and you can distinctly see the full spectrum of its seven colours.

With a sense of joy you walk slowly into the first band of coloured light. This is also like a mist and is of the purest red. You stand and breathe it in as if it were food. Every cell in your body feels invigorated and energized. Just standing there is a very sensual experience and you can't help but notice how beautiful the scenery is and how deliciously soft and inviting the grass is beneath your feet. You know you are supported and loved.

When you feel you have breathed in this red light for long enough, simply continue and move into the next band. This has a golden, orange glow and has a different quality to the red. Have a look at the landscape, perhaps this is different as well. As you stand in this light, just breathing it in, you are infused with warmth and a sense of joy. You feel enthusiastic and hopeful about your life and your mind begins to fill with new creative ideas.

Just remain there as long as feels comfortable and when you are ready, move into the next band of colour. As you step forward you find yourself in a yellow radiance. Everything around you is suffused by it and your body fills with it as you take each new breath.

Here you feel strong in yourself. You know who you are and you are completely unafraid. You are excited about life and very optimistic about what lies ahead of you. You feel cheerful, light and creative and are simply glad to be where you are.

You sense that you hold the sun within and as you absorb this colour, it feeds your inner sun, making it shine more brightly. When it feels right, simply move into the next band of colour.

This is a most beautiful green and the moment you step into it, a great sense of peace and calm envelopes you. Your heart is open and you become aware of the great love you have for all in existence. You do not feel judgemental but rather compassionate and sensitive to all living things. You experience a deep balancing within and in that moment commit to maintaining, as far as possible, a responsible attitude to supporting life positively.

When you have taken in as much green as feels right, you again move to the next band of colour.

This band is peaceful blue. The moment you enter, it's as though you've crossed a bridge into another world. You feel serene and deeply at peace. Whilst you're in this blue light, you remember your life wishes or dreams and you sincerely commit to communicating your truth.

You drink this colour in and feel as nourished and cleansed as if you were being washed through by the clear, sparkling water of a gentle and refreshing waterfall. As soon as you are ready, you leave this band of blue radiance for deepest indigo.

Here you feel elevated and more connected to your intuitive and mystical nature. You may even find yourself in an enchanted forest filled with this indigo light. All your senses are heightened and it is as if you are experiencing many different levels of being all at once. You find that by focusing your attention, you can still discern what is around you and that you are easily able to tap into your wise and intelligent nature. Your open-mindedness unifies all your experiences here and you become aware of the intricate and delicate web that connects all existence.

Allow your imagination to freely explore and only when you are ready, move into the next band of colour, which is a violet-lit landscape where your whole body, mind and spirit feel recharged with a new lightness and purpose. As you take in this violet light, the scenery surrounding you is of a more celestial nature and you can hear the most delicate music.

You feel as if you are in an open-air temple and with great respect and reverence you find an appropriate place to sit quietly. Here you feel lifted to great heights and experience the most profound sense of calm and bliss.

You stay for a while and only decide to leave this place when it feels right to move fully back into the room where you began. Before you do, see yourself passing through each colour that came before, so that you end with the red aspect of the rainbow.

Sense this red in the lower part of your body, grounding you and connecting you completely to where you are. Send the image of a large root of light growing from the red and rooting you deeply in the earth.

Take time to flex your toes and fingers, stretch your body and when it feels right, gently open your eyes. Don't be afraid to see everything as if for the first time.

There will come a time when you will naturally take yourself into your own meditations. You will find that as you explore the depths of your consciousness, stories will simply reveal themselves and you will trust that it is your Higher Self's way of communicating a path to healing for you.

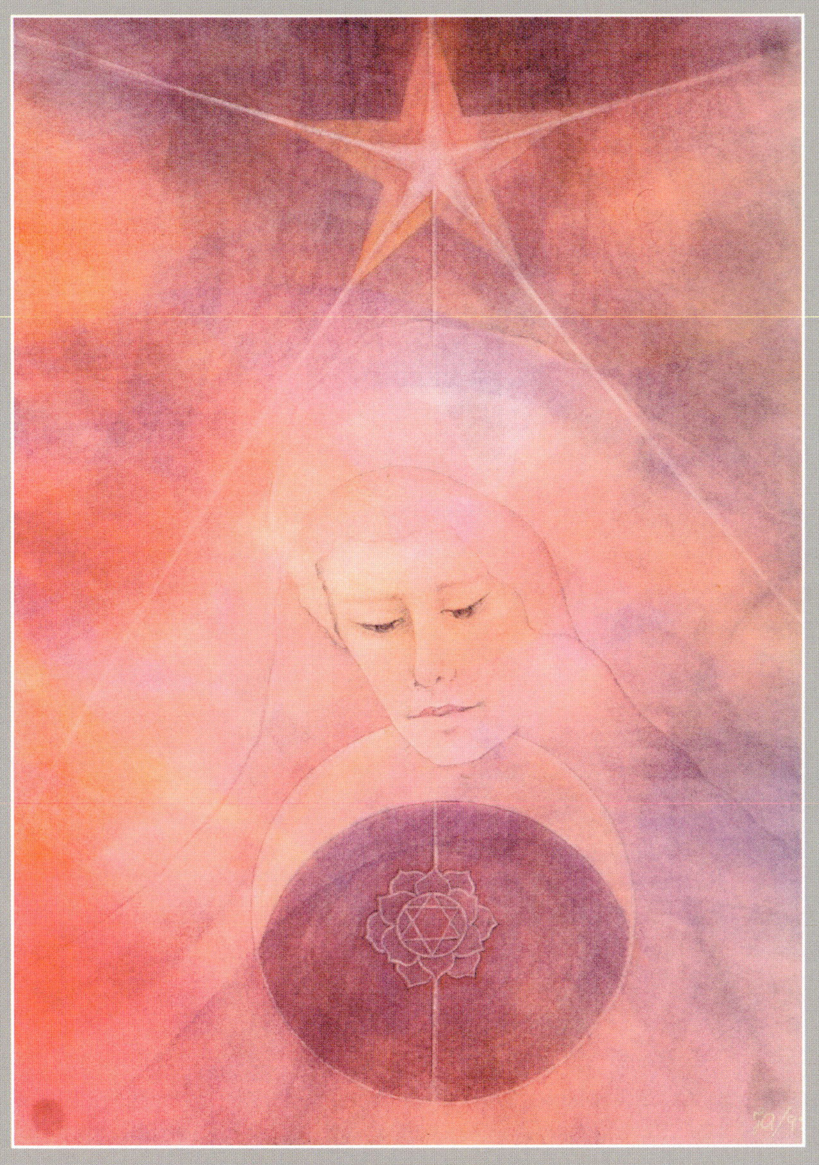

Mother of light

Commit to maintaining a responsible attitude to supporting life positively

CREATIVE MIDWIFERY
Quantum leaping

Creativity cannot be taught. The process of creative unfoldment is like that of giving birth. We need to trust that any difficulty, anticipation, excitement, risk and seeming lack of control will result in the birth of something that is new and has the potential to change us in a profound way.

All the information and technical skill in the world simply serve to inform the head and not the heart. I choose not use the word mind in this instance because my understanding is that mind describes the whole of our energy system with all of its interrelated and interconnected aspects and not just a part of us. Creativity would remain dormant and unexpressed, like a seed without water, unless a third factor came into the situation. This vital intervening force is that of our passion. It is this alchemical marriage of body, mind and spirit that invites creative self-exploration and results in an impassioned and awakened soul.

Creative expression is always about a personal journey and is unique to each soul's experience. Whatever the images, words, mediums or colours we choose to use, enables the expansion of our communication and primarily of those emotions and insights that exist beyond the scope of our reasoning. This free expression of the soul offers us the opportunity to heal and affirm life. Everything we say about ourselves creatively speaks firsthand with authenticity about the movement of our soul. The images and choices we make are deeply significant and can usually be identified with universal, archetypal relevance. It must also be

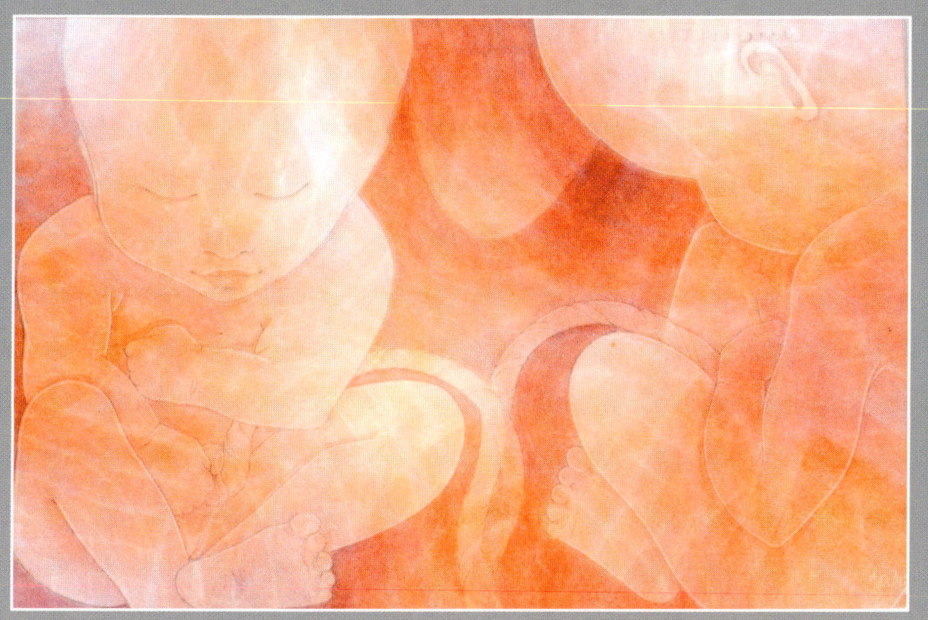

Caliphi – The Twins

Held within the womb of love and wisdom, each unique, each perfection.
Never have we been nor shall we be separated in essence.

recognized that the depth of content in any art work always corresponds to the metaphysical environment in which it is created. This affirms that those who are connected to the subtler realms have a more direct and inner relationship to them. The work reveals itself in its uncensored honesty and this in itself becomes a remedy. The key in any work like this is to allow an instinctive spontaneity without wishing to be correct in any way or desiring approval. It is not available for grading, criticism or validation.

Creative expression is revolutionary and its purpose is to break down out-moded ideas and replace them with radically, life-changing paradigms. This is a transformational process and has a great impact not only at an individual level but also when the expression becomes transpersonal. For example a person may be expressing their grief, sadness, anger etc; and the resulting change can impact other's lives positively as well as their own. Often we speak for others at a time when they are unable to themselves. Creativity through the expression of art cannot be and should not be dismissed to a particular discipline or institutional practice. By its very nature it needs freedom, and when given that, it liberates us from the need to explain.

Creation is our innate connection to all life and as sentient beings we instinctively know where to go and what to change.

The main premise for any facilitator has always been that we can only support and encourage another's exploration, through a commitment to our own. In many ways this has to be an affirming of the individual's freedom of expression and inquiry whatever the variety of mediums or method of practice. Teaching is then primarily about assisting others to gain access to their unrealized potentialities.

The following series of exercises are ones that I have found to be the simplest and most effective both in the studio and via the internet with people across the country.

The tools needed include a set of inexpensive wax crayons, watercolours, acrylic paints in small tubs and an A3 cartridge or watercolour pad. You can get this all at any retail outlet that sells school and office equipment or alternately at an art supplier.

Make a sacred space for yourself that you can always return to. It could be a desk or even a corner of a room. In this place you can build the energy as you re-dedicate yourself on a daily basis to healing and meeting with your highest potential. Lighting a candle before you work links you symbolically to the greater light of who you are. It also allows you to focus on what you are doing.

It's good to meditate before starting and if you are not familiar with this practice just try connecting into the deep silence where you can experience peace and non-judgement. Give yourself at least 10 - 15 minutes for this. If this amount of time is not possible at any point just remember why you are meeting with yourself before you begin to work. Always ask that you be guided by your Higher Self.

I would suggest that on all occasions when working, keep your eyes closed prior to painting or writing, so that you stay connected to the sense of calm within. This is then the way in which you can hold and support yourself if something comes up that doesn't feel too comfortable experientially. Try not to linger when working as this allows your left brain to kick in and distract you. Trust me, it always will!

FIRST EXERCISE

You'll need wax crayons and cartridge paper.

Draw a line down the centre of the paper and on the left side write down your greatest fears, allowing the colours to choose you for each one. Now number them in order of priority ie; greatest to least. Don't ponder, note them and just move on. Once you've done this, put a large colour dot next to each fear, again allowing the colour for each to choose you.

Next, on the right side of the paper, write down the qualities you most admire in others, again allowing the colours that speak loudest. List these from 1 - 10 consecutively, also placing a colour dot next to each one.

By matching the number next to the fear with the corresponding numbered quality, you will see that this is a clear directive from spirit as to how you can begin to heal yourself. [ie; the fear of loneliness – the quality of sharing etc;] If the correspondence is not immediately clear then just accept it and trust that in time it will make sense. The colour dots will also help you to understand that the area within the body that relates directly to the colour of the fear, holds the specific colour key to your healing eg; you may have placed a red dot next to the fear of being abandoned. By working with this colour you have the possibility of unlocking and resolving all those issues that keep the fear locked within your body-mind. Referring back to the chapters on colour would be useful.

When you have finished place this piece of paper up where you can constantly refer to it, giving yourself perhaps one inner attitude project at a time. For example when you may be feeling lonely, rather than sitting around make a conscious effort to visit with someone who may really benefit from your company etc; I also suggest that you re-write these on a smaller format and keep them in your wallet or purse.

SECOND EXERCISE

You will need watercolour paper, a sponge, water and watercolour paints.

Sit quietly, and with your eyes closed, imagine yourself standing in front of a large building. You feel drawn to entering through the main doorway. As you do so, you see a door to your right. Open this and as you enter you close the door behind you to find that the whole room is red. Red furnishings, red paintwork even the air has a redness to it. There's a seat in the middle of the room and as you sit down you begin to remember someone whom you need to forgive or be forgiven by. This very thought brings them in through the door and with a sense of relief you beckon them to your side. Holding their hands in yours you look compassionately into their eyes saying you forgive them or alternately that you need forgiveness. This releases them of any further difficulty between you. This may also include someone who has passed on.

Now gently open your eyes and wet the paper with the sponge and begin painting immediately, not losing the emotion you have from the visualization. Don't judge or criticise what you do and simply let your feelings describe themselves through the colour. Again, don't stop to ponder or review what you have done and once you have finished just put down the paintbrush.

I suggest repeating this exercise daily until you feel you have met with all those whom you feel have wronged you or you have wronged in some way. You may experience anger, frustration etc; just let it be and keep painting. Please journal your feelings if this feels appropriate. Sometimes you may feel the need to write on the painting as well. It is not important what you write but that you do so spontaneously and without censoring the words that need to find expression. Allow yourself the freedom to also write with your left hand if you are right handed and alternatively with your right if you are left handed.

THIRD EXERCISE

You'll require watercolour paper and paints, sponge and water.

Begin again with quiet time, focus on your belly area and bring in thoughts of softness and peace with each inbreath. With each outbreath imagine letting go of all difficulty and blockages. Allow nothing to distract you and keep bringing your attention back to the belly. Continue this for at least ten in and out breaths.

Gradually imagine that you are being surrounded and infused with the most delicate pale pink light and with each inbreath you become more and more radiant. This fills you with the most beautiful sense of lightness and gratitude and offers you a glimpse and awareness of the greater You. Stay connected to this sensation in the way of surrendering to it rather than wanting to control it.

Gently, and without any inner expectation open your eyes and begin to paint. Allow the brush to move where it will and the colours to choose you. Don't hesitate or stop at all till it feels right.

You may now write on a separate piece of paper with coloured crayons, the feelings you are experiencing. Again simply date and sign both works and put them away. Please repeat this for a couple of days.

You do not need to understand what the colours mean. We can do this but it is not necessary as they always speak for themselves and are a true reflection of exactly how one is at that given moment. One can get lost in the left brain trying to decipher the choice of colour. There are obviously situations where it is very helpful to decode colour, but in this instance creative expression through spontaneous colour choice is essentially cathartic.

For all processing exercises it is important to drink as much water as possible, particularly during and after, as the process can be tiring and always detoxifying and the water will help to flush the toxins out. I also recommend that when one works in this way that there is a little time after the exercises to be quiet and just re-group before going into the rest of the day.

FOURTH EXERCISE

You will need watercolour paints and paper, a little water and a photograph of yourself that you like.

This is a wonderful exercise in letting go of preconceived notions and ideas of yourself and the way you would like to be seen.

Having found a photo that you enjoy looking at, place it upside-down at the very top left hand corner of the page. Resist the temptation to turn it the correct way till the exercise is completely finished. Also please don't scrutinize the details of the picture and rather paint as if you were a child given the freedom to use any colours they choose in any way that feels right.

Now sit quietly and follow your breathing till it becomes regular and your body feels relaxed. Remind yourself that this is time for you alone and within this space you are safe and protected. Consciously let go of the need to do anything in a certain way and when you are ready begin to paint quite loosely what you see in front of you. The child in you may well want to use an interesting combination of colours and exaggerate shapes, let it. Allow your hand to move quickly and don't stop till there is an inner directive to do so.

I always suggest walking away for a little while, once the work is complete, just to distance yourself from its energy. When the time is right, turn your painting around and place it where you can easily view it.

This picture can be very evocative and you may laugh or for that matter cry when you look at the image. Usually I find that what has been depicted so innocently is an energy print of one's essence at the time.

Please keep the paintings dated and labeled so that they may later serve as a form of journal, if needs be. Often this way of working allows us to let go of things more easily and we are less precious about needing to hold onto the past.

FIFTH EXERCISE

You will need a set of acrylic paints, masking tape, cartridge pad, kitchen towel and water. In this exercise you will need to put paint into a palette or onto some paper so that you can dip your fingers directly into the colours. If you have little tubs of colour all the better.

Begin by centreing yourself. Simply observe your breath as it passes through your nostrils to your lungs and back again. Sense the way it is cool when breathed in and warm when breathed out. Go more deeply and become aware of its life giving properties as it flows through you and then become aware of the toxins that are carried and then released as it passes out of you. When you feel relaxed and ready it is important that you just start to paint with your fingers.

As in the previous exercises allow the colours to choose you and listen to where the energy wants to go as you move your hand across the paper. Here you are free to do whatever feels right, whether its smudging, scratching, blending, building up texture etc; You will probably begin to notice that as you handle the paint it begins to warm on your fingers and a special relationship is established.

This exercise can be very energizing and releasing and I would encourage you to do this whenever you feel blocked, frustrated, angry or low in energy. As mentioned before it's good to drink water particularly after these exercises as it helps to eliminate toxins that may have been released during the process.

All these exercises are designed to be worked with at home and by the individual. They have also been used in larger group contexts very successfully and in these situations its necessary to give quiet time after in order to digest and let go of any residual feelings in order to move to the next process freely. There are obviously instances when working more deeply with the symbols and images that emerge is important and in these cases one should seek professional guidance and support. It can be incredibly positive and constructive to do this work in conjunction with therapy, essentially because of its right brain and intuitive content.

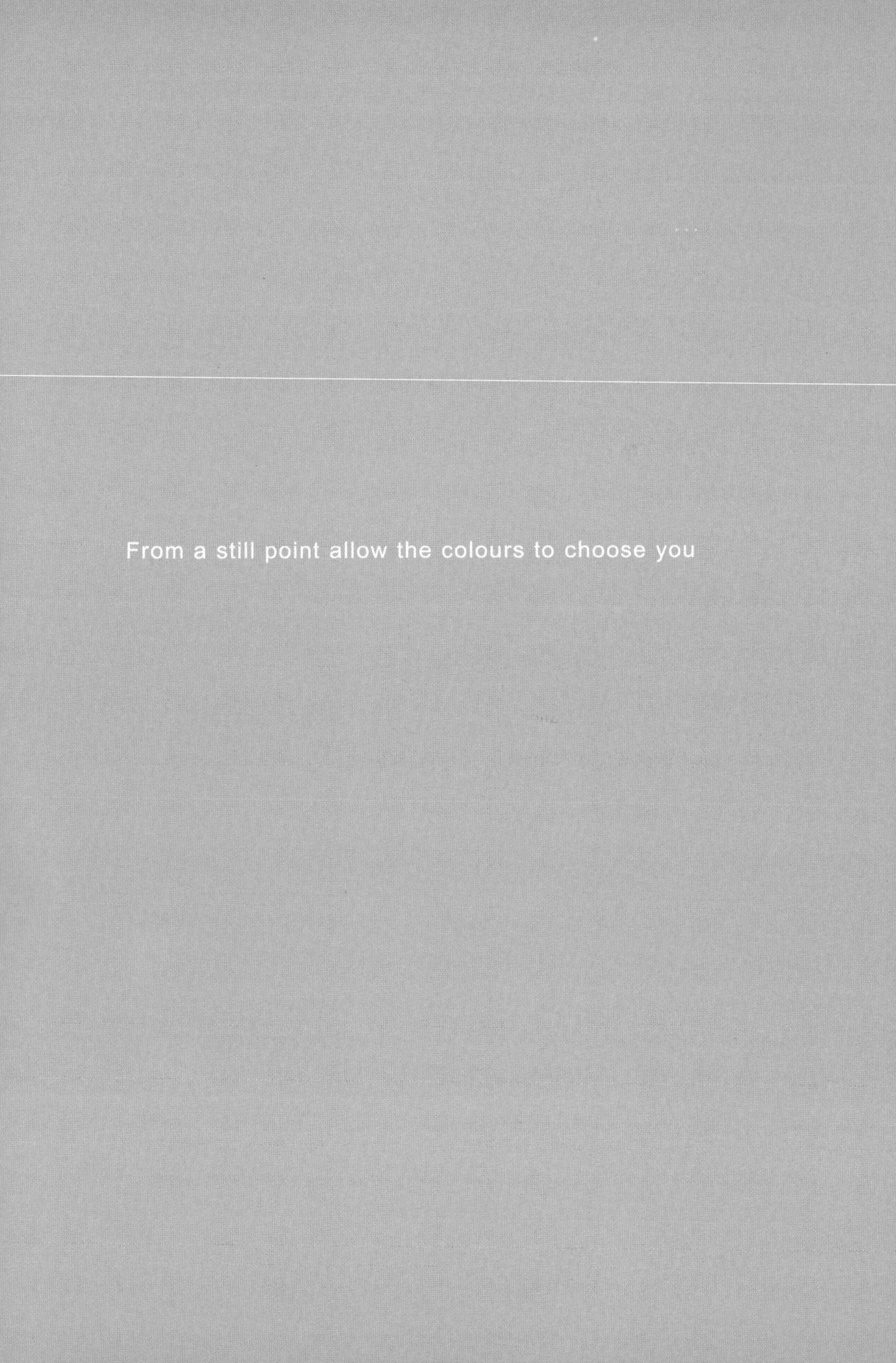
From a still point allow the colours to choose you

SUGGESTED READING

The Miracle of Colour Healing
Aura Soma Therapy as the Mirror of the Soul
Vicky Wall
Published by Aquarian
ISBN 1-85538-289-X

Colour Healing
A practical guide to understanding the healing power of colour
Lilian Verner Bonds
Published by Vermilion
ISBN 0-09-181506-1

The Power of Colour
How it can reduce fatigue, relieve monotony, enhance sexuality...and more
Faber Birren
Published by Citadel Press
ISBN 0-8065-1857-X

Sun over Mountain
A course in creative imagination
Jessica Macbeth
Published by Gateway Books, Bath
ISBN 0-946551-67-7

Living on Light
The Source of Nourishment for the New Millenium
Jasmuheen
Published by KOHA
ISBN -3-929512-33-5

Art as Medicine
Creating a Therapy of the Imagination
Shaun McNiff
Published by Piatkus
ISBN 0-7499-1341-X

The Awakened Eye
A companion volume to the Zen of Seeing
Frederick Franck
Published by Wildwood House
ISBN 0- 7045- 0380-8

Colour Healing
Thorsons Principles of-
Ambika Wauters and Gerry Thompson
Published by Thorsons
ISBN 0-7225-3340-3

Autobiography of a Yogi
By Paramhansa Yogananda
Published by Crystal and Clarity
ISBN-1-56589-108-2

USEFUL COLOUR, ART, AND ASSOCIATE THERAPIES WEB SITES

www.aura-soma.net

www.crystal-healing.org

www.internationalassociationofcolour.com

www.arttherapy.co.za/associations.htm

www.malacti.com/colourtherapyinternational

www.mymandala.net/workshop.htm

www.artofliving.org

www.link-up.co.za

www.bodyandmind.co.za

www.iriscolour.co.uk

www.luminati.com/crystalhtm/

www.mostinnermost.co.za

www.colourtherapyhealing.com

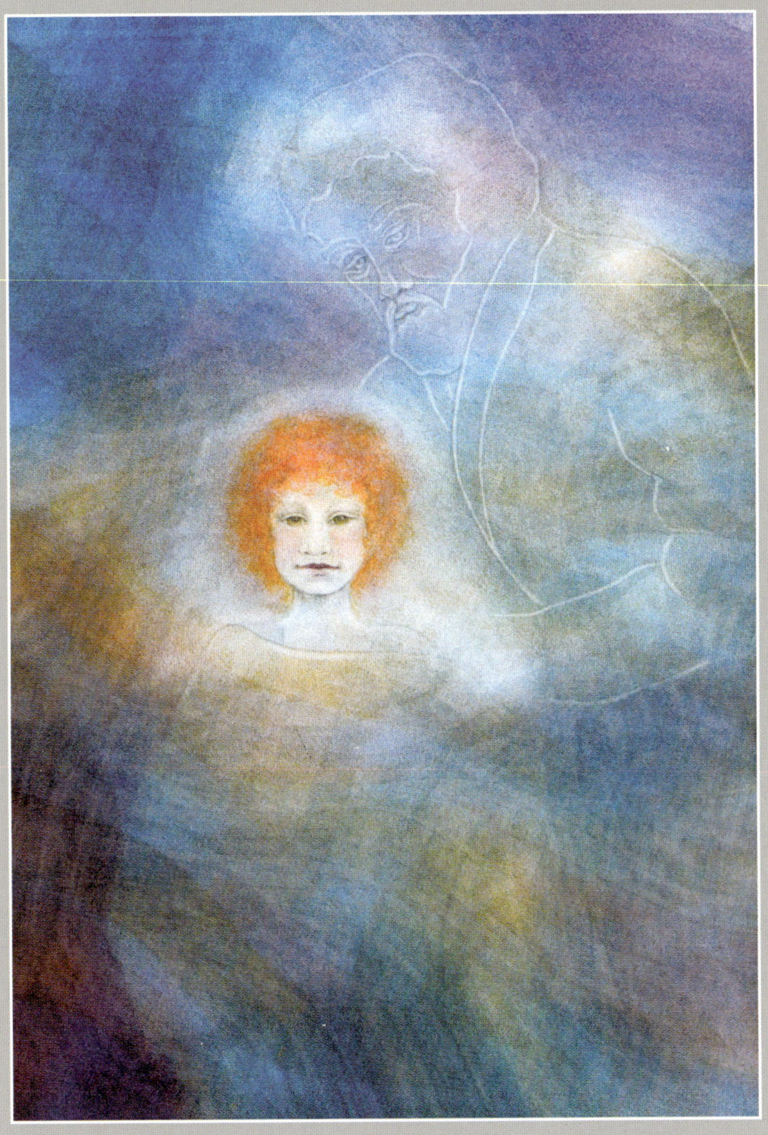

Healing Hands

Lest we forget how we are guided and healed by invisible hands as loved ones and teachers patiently stand by offering their gifts with such tenderness.

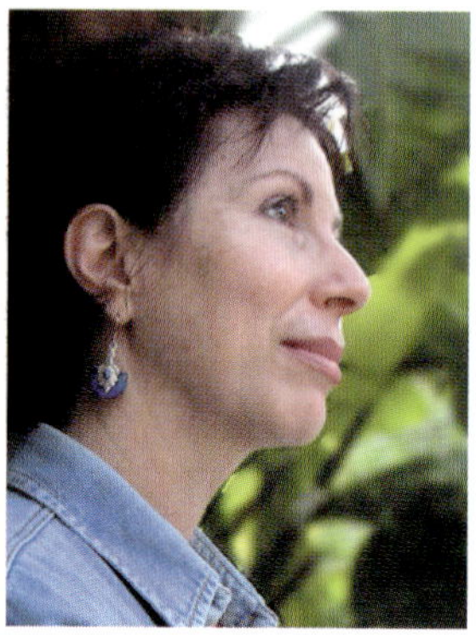

Fiona Almeleh, mystic, visionary and sensitive, lives the life of colour she was born to explore and teach.

Born in Zimbabwe, Fiona studied fine art in Natal, South Africa. She worked as a freelance artist and illustrator in CapeTown before moving to Britain in the mid 70's. Here she extended her work to include all aspects of book design and production and at the same time embarked on an intense spiritual journey of self - exploration.

Following the birth of her children, Aaron and Ilana, she continued book illustrating as well as designing and making silver jewellery. Her creative spirit then turned to oil painting, veil painting and embroidery sculpture. Here the deepest sense of her joy and ever unfolding understanding of the wonders of life became the expression of her work.

Fiona has exhibited both locally in South Africa and abroad in England and Scotland, mainly in one-woman shows. In December 1999 she was invited as a guest exhibitor at the World Parliament of Religions.

Whatever medium, her projects are always unplanned and spontaneous. Her work commits to the inner process of evolving, inviting others to reconnect to that part of the human psyche that dares to explore and believe in the possibility of a journey of magnificence.

Fiona has been facilitating creative exploration and healing through colour for the past eleven years with both adults and children. She works as an energy intuitive, artist, colour healer and teacher and is registered with NHA (National Healers Association).

Her articles and interviews have appeared in several national and international magazines, newspapers and journals. She has been a guest on South African radio and TV programmes including Top Billing, Tabloid, Options, Free Spirit and the international series Innertainment.

Some of Fiona's work may be viewed on www.southafricanartists.com/home/FionaAlmeleh, as well as www.naturalhealth.co.za under practitioners, colour and art therapy.

Colour

Colour dances and moves, filtering clouds of luminosity
through every level of what we create.
Words of love speak the palest pink as they infuse
each cell with warmth and nurturing.
Softest orange reminds and excites as it spreads its glow,
lightly awakening spiritual and physical intimacy.
Yellow of the sunniest radiance causes us to smile at the joy
and creativity that have been given the freedom to flow and
flourish as we say yes to life's gifts.
Green of such delicacy illumines the connective fibres that
unite us with each other and all life.
Saphire blue surrounds and protects as it offers a bridge
that spans other realities, calling forth honesty and integrity
through communication as we speak without fear.
Velvety indigo holds us in its sacred womb of clarity, insight
and universal wisdom.
Violet and magenta merge, gently pulsing the higher
purpose of each man , woman and child as we all begin to
experience the miraculous and transcend the ordinary.
Humankind is cocooned in a coral translucence, pregnant
with potential and like all great soul stories this is spun from
the finest threads of purest white light.

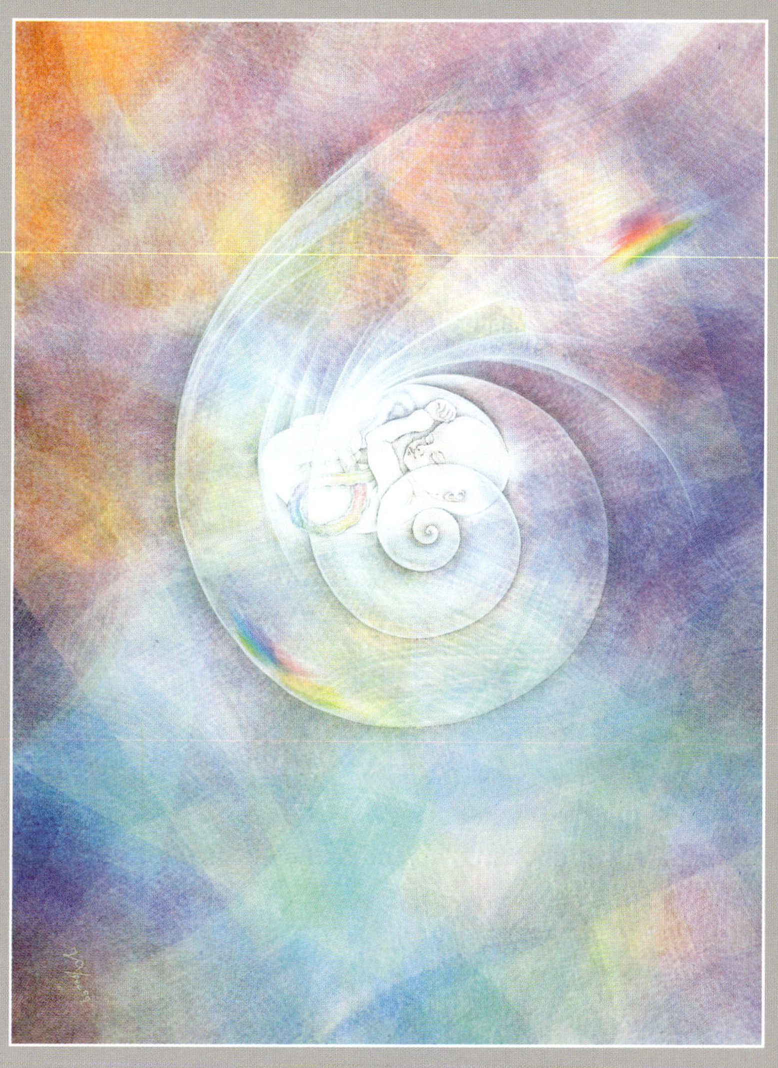

Of Love and Light

Also available by Fiona Almeleh

A THREAD RUNS THROUGH IT
STORIES, STITCHES AND POEMS FROM THE HEART

ISBN 0-620-29908-8

All rights reserved.
No part of this publications may be reproduced or transmitted in any form or by any means, electronic or mechanical including photocopy, or any information storage and retrieval system without the permission in writing from the publisher.

Fiona Almeleh wishes to thank:

Warren Nelson, Carol Nelson, Susan Emily Pitt and ABC Press